Viol[illegible]

PRACTICE MATH TESTS FOR New York City SHSAT SPECIALIZED HIGH SCHOOL ADMISSIONS TEST VOLUME 2

5 full-length math section SHSAT practice exams with solutions

NAMISTAI BOOKS

Namistai Books, the publishing division of Namistai LLC, works with the best authors to produce high quality educational materials for all levels. To see everything we have to offer, visit us at http://www.namistai.com.

If you find an error in any of our books, please email us at **errata@namistai.com** (put "Book error" in the subject line). We will make sure to correct the error in the next printing, and send you a small souvenir to acknowledge your efforts. To check the list of all errata that have been found in this and previous volumes, please visit **http://www.namistai.com/books/shsat/errata**.

If you need to contact us regarding volume purchases of our materials (we provide significant discounts!), or for any other reason, email **contact@namistai.com**.

If you have any questions for Mrs. Violetta Dubinina, the author of this book, please go to the web page for this book, at **http://www.namistai.com/books/shsat/**, and click "Contact the author".

January 2015 Edition

Table of Contents

"To the Reader" from Volume 1

If you are reading this book, you have presumably decided to apply for admission to New York City's specialized high schools. This is a laudable and serious decision. You likely understand that admission to these schools is highly competitive, but if you stay confident and work hard to prepare for it, your chances of admission will improve.

First and foremost, you should know that the specialized high schools look for students who are very enthusiastic about learning and who are curious and diligent in every subject area.

The biggest challenge associated with the SHSAT is that it does not just test your knowledge (in fact, most problems require only basic knowledge), but that it tests your ability to understand and interpret text, think logically, look for non-standard solution methods, use spatial reasoning, answer intermediate questions on the way to a solution, and separate necessary and extraneous information. The test also requires students to work quickly, without breaks, with intense concentration and the good judgment to skip difficult problems and return to them at the end.

How should you go about learning how to do all that? The best way, as cliché as it might be, is through practice. This collection of practice tests is specifically tailored for those students who need additional practice on the part of the test that many consider the most "scary": the Math section. The actual test consists of two parts – Verbal and Math. The Math section contains 50 multiple-choice questions that must be solved in 75 minutes. That means that your total time to read, understand, and solve a single problem is just 1.5 minutes.

To practice in the most efficient way possible, do a single test, strictly adhering to the 75 minute time limit. Then check your answers against the provided answers. Make sure to carefully go over the solutions to problems that you did incorrectly or skipped. A week later, **do the same test** again. Analyze your work: did you remember ways to solve problems? Are you repeating the same errors? If all is well, move on to the next test the following week. In the 10 weeks that it will take you to go through these tests, you will definitely see improvements in both your ability and confidence.

Wishing you success on the SHSAT,
Violetta Dubinina

To The Reader (Added for Volume 2)

If you've purchased this book, chances are you have already made the first step towards success on the SHSAT by thinking through and solving all the problems from Volume 1. You are now equipped with a variety of solution strategies, and a much better understanding of the material.

Now you have 5 more practice exams in your possession. What for? An SHSAT exam demands not just an understanding of the problems and an ability to solve them, but also speed — the exam time is very limited.

These additional practice tests will improve your ability to solve the problems quickly and will allow you to save time that you can spend on the more involved questions from the Verbal section.

As you practice the exams from this volume, make sure that you keep track of the time. Note each problem that takes significantly more time than the 1.5 minute average needed to complete the entire test in time, and understand what's slowing you down, so you can think of ways to improve that particular skill. If you encounter particularly difficult problems, try skipping them and coming back to them later — many students find that a second look at a problem makes solving it a lot easier.

If you solved all the problems in the first volume, you'll also notice that some problems in this volume seem similar. However, those problems have been modified in various subtle, but significant ways, and if you make a conscious note of these differences, you'll be much more aware of your own body of knowledge.

After practicing these tests, you should feel that the process of solving is less stressful, and more enjoyable, which should lead to an increase in confidence and great results on the actual test.

Stay confident and succeed!
Violetta Dubinina

Acknowledgements

The author wishes to recognize readers **William Xiang**, **Rohan Suri**, **Ben Bae, Erik Engquist**, and **Ahmed Chuhan** for the suggestions and corrections they have provided for this book.

SHSAT Practice Math Test 6

SHSAT PRACTICE TEST 6

PART 2 — MATHEMATICS

Suggested Time — 75 Minutes

50 QUESTIONS

---

51. 13% of some number N is equal to 72. What is 26% of the same number?

A. 18
B. 36
C. 38
D. 108
E. 144

---

52. What is the volume of a cube, in cubic centimeters, if its surface area is 600 cm^2?

F. 216 cm^3
G. 360 cm^3
H. 420 cm^3
J. 568 cm^3
K. 1000 cm^3

53. What is the average of all integers between – 7 and 9, inclusive?

A. –2
B. –1
C. 0
D. 1
E. 8.5

---

54. The lengths of all sides of a triangle are integers greater than 3. What is the smallest possible perimeter of the triangle?

F. 12
G. 13
H. 14
J. 15
K. 17

55.

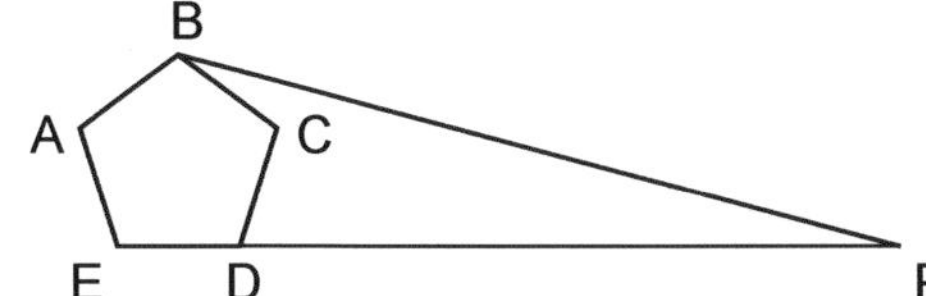

ABCDE is a regular pentagon. If $\angle CBP = 20°$, and $\overline{EDP}$ is a line segment, Find the degree measure of $\angle BPD$.

A. 10°
B. 12°
C. 14°
D. 16°
E. 18°

---

56. $0.2 \times 5 + 10 \div 0.1 =$

F. 20.1
G. 2
H. 11
J. 101
K. 110

---

57. Round 0.91919191919 to the nearest thousandth.

A. 0.9
B. 0.910
C. 0.919
D. 0.920
E. 0.912

---

58. For how many integers a is it true that $a^2 - 8$ is a negative number?

F. 0
G. 2
H. 5
J. 7
K. 8

---

59. M, N and K are three consecutive even numbers. Which of the following statements is **always** true?

A. $M \times N \times K > 0$
B. $M \times N \times K < 0$
C. $M + N + K = 2$
D. $(3M + 7N + 5K)$ is even
E. $(M \times N \times K + 1)$ is even

---

60. The 3–digit number 105 has a digit sum of $1 + 0 + 5 = 6$. How many different 3–digit numbers, including 105, have a digit sum of 6?

F. 21
G. 19
H. 17
J. 16
K. 15

61. Tickets for a play cost $3 for children and $10 for adults. A group of 25 people paid a total of $201 for tickets to the play. How many children were there in a group?

A. 20
B. 18
C. 16
D. 12
E. 7

62.

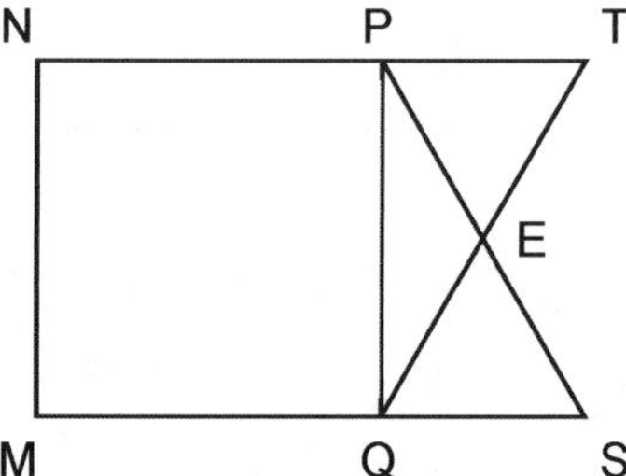

MNPQ is a square, QT = 6, PT = 3. Find the area of the square MNPQ.

F. 27
G. 32
H. 36
J. 38
K. None of these

63. There are 24 students in the class. Which of the following could be the ratio of boys to girls in this class?

A. 1 : 12
B. 2 : 3
C. 3 : 4
D. 5 : 7
E. 7 : 4

64. If it takes 5 pipes 2 hours to fill 2 pools and they output water at the same rate, how many hours will it take 1 pipe to fill 1 pool?

F. 2 hours
G. 3 hours
H. 4 hours
J. 5 hours
K. 10 hours

65. If the sum of two prime numbers is divisible by 7 and is a perfect square, what is a possible product of these numbers?

A. 10
B. 38
C. 94
D. 123
E. 156

66. A six–sided die with sides numbered 1 through 6 is tossed 2 times. What is the probability that the product of the two toss results will be even?

F. 0.2
G. 0.25
H. 0.6
J. 0.75
K. 0.8

67. If $b^{\triangle} = 3 - 5b$, what is the value of $(-2)^{\triangle}$?

A. −13
B. −18
C. −7
D. 13
E. −30

68. On a test with 30 questions, Ron got 6 questions wrong. What is his score expressed as a percentage?

F. 20%
G. 60%
H. 75%
J. 80%
K. 85%

69.

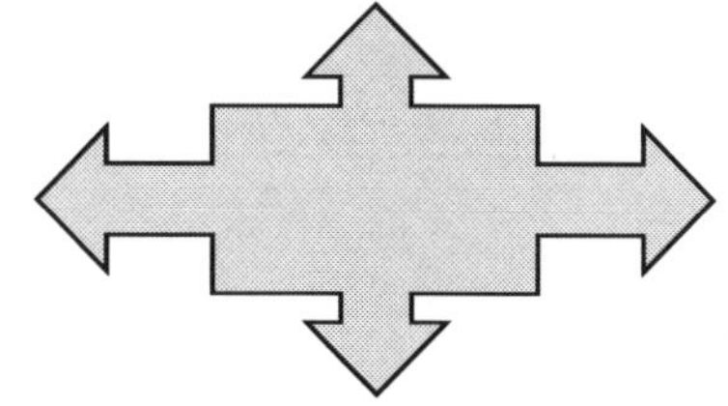

How many lines of symmetry does the figure above have?

A. 1
B. 2
C. 4
D. 6
E. None of these

70. 35% of a class voted to go to the museum. If 7 students chose to go to the museum, how many students are there in the class?

F. 35
G. 30
H. 25
J. 24
K. 20

71. 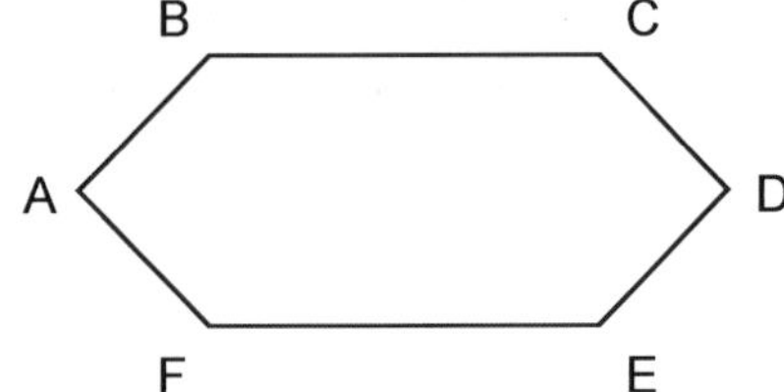

In the polygon above, the degree measures of interior angles A and D are the same. The degree measures of interior angles B, C, E, and F are equal to each other, and 15° more than the measure of angle A. Find the measure of angle E.

A. 100°
B. 120°
C. 125°
D. 130°
E. 135°

72. If $2a = 3b$, and $6b = 5c$ what is the ratio of a to c?

F. 5 : 4
G. 3 : 5
H. 4 : 5
J. 5 : 3
K. None of these

73. By what percentage is 70 less than 200?

A. 10%
B. 38%
C. 65%
D. 70%
E. 140%

74. Katie is 2 years younger than her brother. In 12 years, her brother will be twice as old as she is now. How old is Katie now?

F. 10
G. 12
H. 14
J. 15
K. 16

75. ← ↖ ↑ ↗ → ↘ ↓ ↙ ← ↖ ↑ ↗ → ↘ ↓ ↙ ...

If the pattern above is continued, what will be its 55th term?

A. ←
B. ↓
C. ↑
D. ↗
E. ↘

76. Find the average of $(3x - 5)$, $(x + 2)$, and $(2x + 6)$.

F. $2x - 1$
G. $6x + 3$
H. $6x - 3$
J. $2x + 1$
K. $3x - 1$

77.

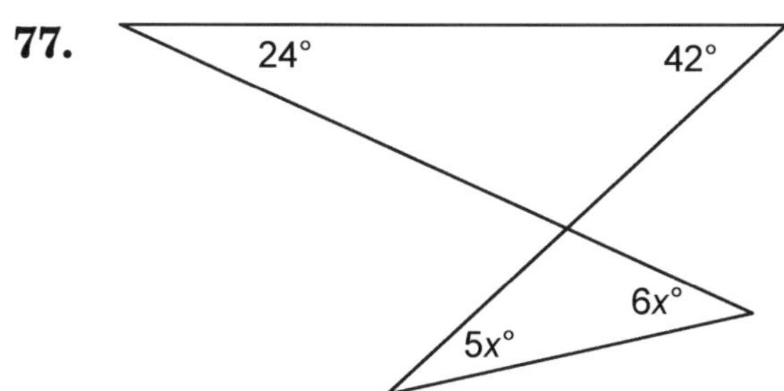

Find x.

A. 3°
B. 4°
C. 5°
D. 6°
E. 8°

78. What is the smallest positive integer that can be added to 27,983 to make the result divisible by 9?

F. 1
G. 2
H. 6
J. 7
K. 9

79. n pens cost d dollars. How many pens you can buy for p dollars?

A. d / np
B. pd / n
C. np / d
D. nd / p
E. ndp

80. $5 \div 0.1 - 8 \div 0.2 \times 0.5 + 6 \div 2 =$

F. 33
G. 23
H. −12
J. −13
K. None of these

81. What is the surface area of a cube if its volume is 125 cm^3?

A. 250 cm^2
B. 150 cm^2
C. 124 cm^2
D. 100 cm^2
E. 625 cm^2

82. How many positive integers between 100 and 300 contain at least one digit 7?

F. 20
G. 38
H. 39
J. 40
K. 47

83. If T and P are both negative numbers, which statement is always false?

A. $P - T > 0$
B. $P + T > 0$
C. $P + T = 2P$
D. $2P - T = 0$
E. $T - P > 0$

84. Two triangles **cannot** have __ common points.

F. 1
G. 2
H. 5
J. 6
K. 7

85. If $t^4 = 1600$, between which two integers does t lie?

A. 5 and 6
B. 6 and 7
C. 12 and 13
D. 39 and 40
E. 41 and 42

86. 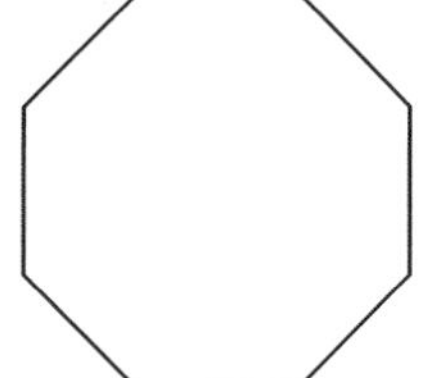

What is the degree measure of the smallest angle between two lines of symmetry of a regular octagon?

F. 12.5°
G. 20°
H. 22.5°
J. 30°
K. 45°

87. If a circle is inscribed into a square with the side of 4 inches, what is the distance between the vertex of the square and the point on the circle closest to it?

A. 2
B. $\sqrt{2}$
C. $2\sqrt{2}$
D. $2\sqrt{2} - 1$
E. $2\sqrt{2} - 2$

88.

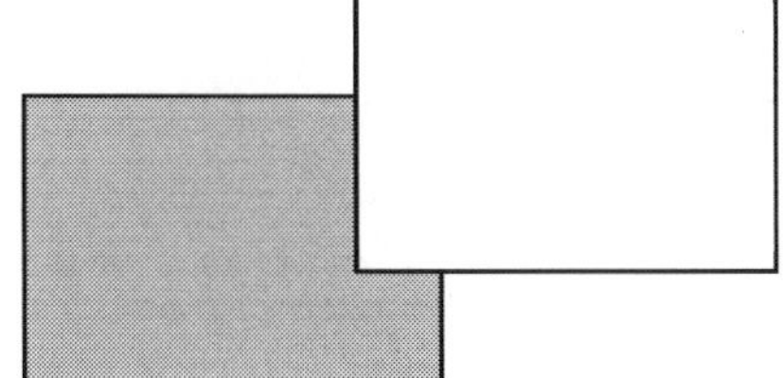

Two congruent rectangles 4 in by 6 in overlap each other. If the shaded area is 20 in^2, what is the area of the hidden part of the shaded rectangle?

F. 12 in^2
G. 8 in^2
H. 6 in^2
J. 4 in^2
K. Cannot be determined

89. What is the area of the circle ($A = \pi r^2$) that passes through the point $(-1, 1)$ and whose center lies at the origin?

A. 2π
B. 3π
C. 4π
D. 5π
E. π

90. Steve entered the elevator at a certain floor. The elevator moved up 7 floors, then down 8 floors, and then up 3 floors. On which floor did Steve initially enter the elevator, if he is now on the 10th floor?

F. 15
G. 9
H. 8
J. 6
K. 4

91. 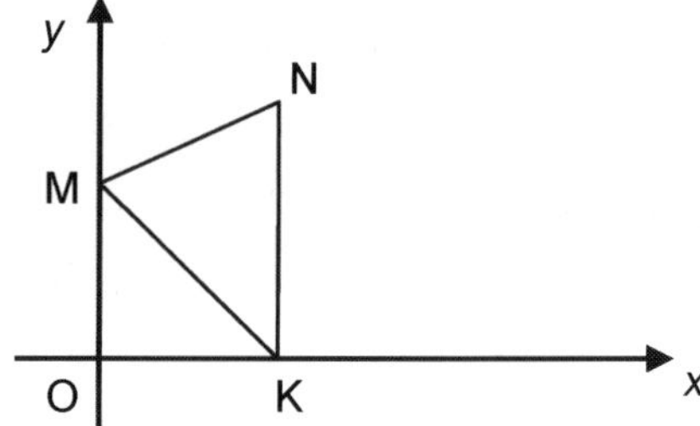

If NK ⊥ x–axis, OM = OK, and MK = NK, find the measure of angle MNK.

A. 75°
B. 68°
C. 67.5°
D. 65.5°
E. 62°

92. If $x^2y^3z^3 < 0$, which statement must be true?

F. $xy > 0$
G. $yz < 0$
H. $xz < 0$
J. $xyz < 0$
K. $x < 0$

93. $\frac{2a - 1}{a + 2} = \frac{5}{3}$. Find a.

A. 9
B. 11
C. 12
D. 13
E. 14

94. If $v^2 = 16$, and $w^2 = 49$, what is the largest possible difference between w and v?

F. 12
G. 11
H. 9
J. 7
K. 3

95. 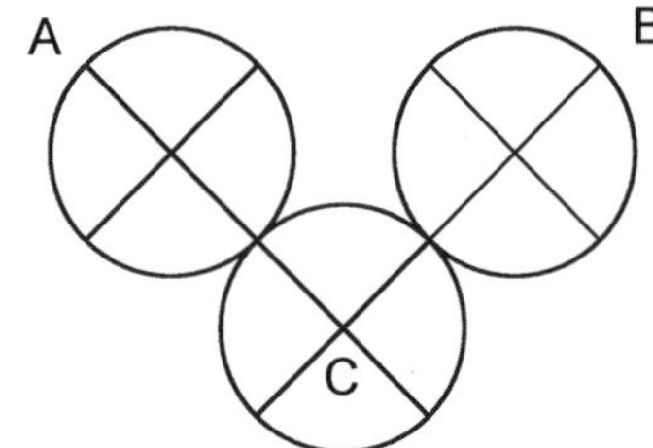

Three congruent circles with radii 2 cm are tangent to each other and divided into 4 congruent parts, as shown above. Find the distance AB.

A. $8\sqrt{2}$
B. $6\sqrt{2}$
C. $6\sqrt{3}$
D. $4\sqrt{2}$
E. $4\sqrt{3}$

96. The ratio of A to B is 4 to 7. What is the ratio of $(A + B)$ to $(B - A)$?

F. 3 : 4
G. 6 : 5
H. 11 : 7
J. 11 : 3
K. Cannot be determined

97. $4x = 3y$, $2y = z$, $6z = v$, $7v = 8w$, and the numbers x, y, z, v, and w are positive. Which of the numbers is the largest?

A. x
B. y
C. z
D. v
E. w

98. The area of a square is equal to the area of a rectangle. If the side of the square is an integer, which of the following pairs of numbers could be the dimensions of the rectangle?

F. 17, 15
G. 15, 14
H. 16, 12
J. 12, 3
K. None of the above

99. The average of a and b is 3 times larger than the average of c and d. If the average of a, b, c, and d is 10, what is the average of c and d?

A. 20
B. 10
C. 8
D. 5
E. cannot be determined

100.

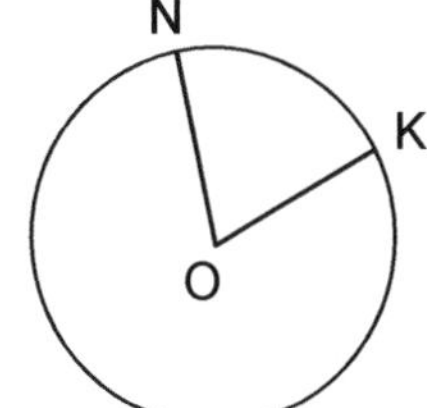

If the region NOK contains 20% of the circle, what is the degree measure of the angle NOK?

F. 80°
G. 76°
H. 75°
J. 72°
K. 60°

SHSAT Practice Math Test 7

SHSAT PRACTICE TEST 7

PART 2 — MATHEMATICS

Suggested Time — 75 Minutes

50 QUESTIONS

---

51. If you divide a five–digit number by a one–digit number, what is the largest possible remainder you can get?

A. 9
B. 8
C. 6
D. 5
E. 4

---

52. What is the midpoint of the line segment KL on the number line, if K (–0.3) and L (0.1)?

F. –0.25
G. –0.2
H. –0.1
J. 0
K. 0.05

53. $(0.2)^{-3} \div (0.1)^{-4} =$

A. 0.25
B. 0.0125
C. $\frac{5}{8}$
D. $\frac{1}{8}$
E. None of these

---

54. A trail mix consists of 2 pounds of dry fruits costing \$1.30 per pound and 3 pounds of nuts costing \$3.60 per pound. What is the price of 1 pound of the trail mix?

F. \$0.98
G. \$1.25
H. \$2.40
J. \$2.68
K. \$3.60

55. 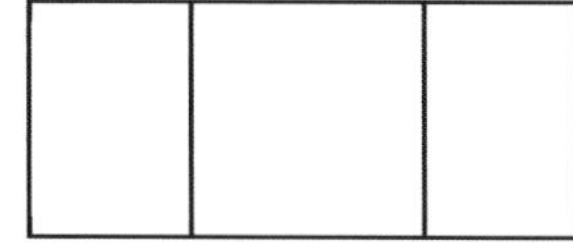

Two congruent 5 by 3 rectangles overlap as shown in the image and form a square. Find the area of the entire figure.

A. 30
B. 28
C. 25
D. 21
E. 12

56. If a faucet can fill a tub in 10 minutes, how long will it take to fill $\frac{1}{2}$ of the tub?

F. 20 min
G. 15 min
H. 8 min
J. 5 min
K. 2 min

57. The operation ❄ is defined for all nonzero numbers by a ❄ $b = a^2 - b$
Find (2 ❄ –5) ❄ –1.

A. 82
B. 47
C. 42
D. 0
E. –9

58. The volume of a cube is 64 in^3. What is the volume of the cube in ft^3?

F. 64 ft^3
G. 4 ft^3
H. 1 ft^3
J. $\frac{1}{3}$ ft^3
K. $\frac{1}{27}$ ft^3

59.

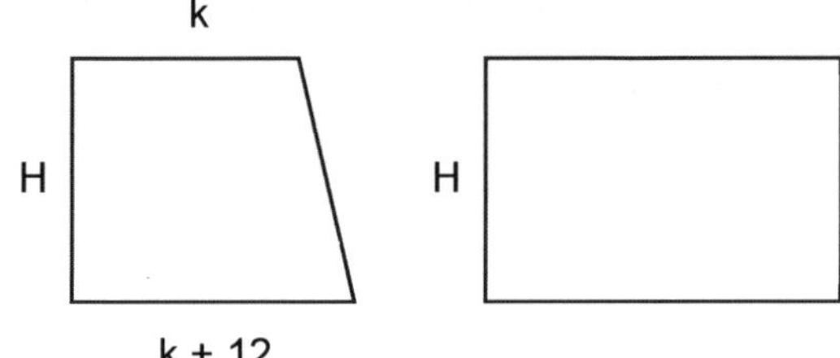

A trapezoid and a rectangle have the same height H. The area of the rectangle is equal to the area of the trapezoid. If the bases of the trapezoid are k and $(k + 12)$, what is the width of the rectangle in terms of k?

A. $k + 3$
B. $k + 5$
C. $k + 6$
D. $k + 12$
E. $2k + 12$

---

60. If the reciprocal of the number is 4 times the number itself, what is the number?

F. 4
G. 2
H. 1
J. $\frac{1}{2}$
K. 0

---

61. The median of a set of 22 consecutive numbers is 26.5. Find the median of the first 11 numbers of this set.

A. 21
B. 20
C. 19
D. 18
E. 17

---

62. If $p > 5$ and $q - 10p = 0$, which of the following must be true?

F. $q > 0.5$
G. $q > 1.5$
H. $q < 0.5$
J. $q < 28$
K. $q > 50$

---

63. It is known that $x > y$, $z < y$, $w < z$, and $w > t$. If x, y, z, w and t are positive numbers, which one is the smallest?

A. x
B. y
C. z
D. w
E. t

64. $(5^6 + 5^6 + 5^6) \div (5^4 + 5^4 + 5^4) =$

F. 25^{10}

G. 625^2

H. 25

J. 5^{24}

K. 25^2

65.

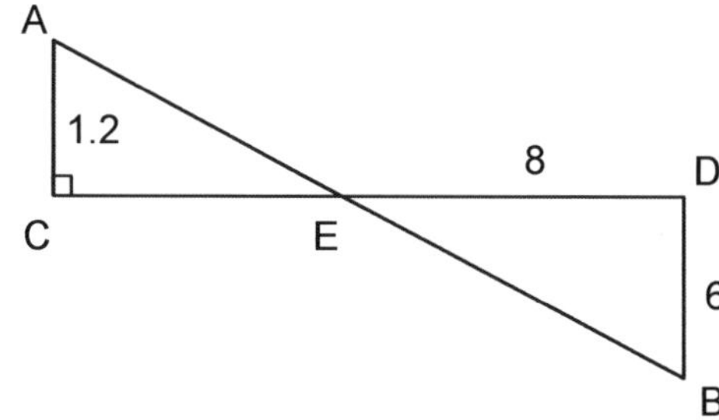

If AC‖BD, AC = 1.2, DE = 8, and BD = 6, find AE.

A. 2.5

B. $\frac{8}{5}$

C. 5

D. 4

E. 2

66. $(4^3)(8^2) = 2^x$. What is x?

F. 4

G. 5

H. 6

J. 12

K. 14

67. Find the largest factor of 1260 which is not divisible by 6.

A. 630

B. 315

C. 280

D. 63

E. 35

68. $(\sqrt{11} + \sqrt{11})^2 =$

F. 242

G. 121

H. 44

J. 22

K. 11

69.

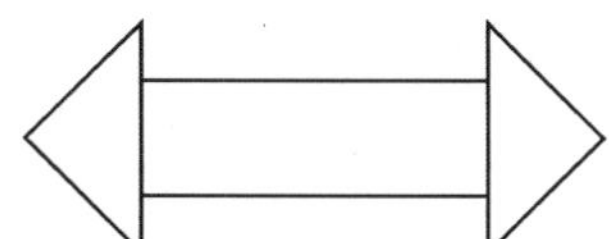

The figure above consists of a rectangle and two right isosceles triangles. The dimensions of the rectangle are 8 inches by 2 inches, and the hypotenuse of each triangle is 4 inches. Find the area of the entire figure.

A. 32 in^2

B. 30 in^2

C. 24 in^2

D. 20 in^2

E. 16 in^2

70. $32 \div (-8) \times 2 - 24 \div 4 \times (-3) - 1 =$

F. −27
G. −25
H. −20
J. 9
K. 27

71.

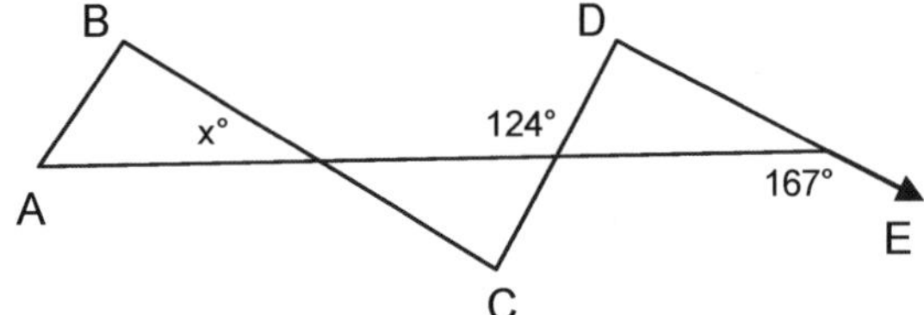

Find the measure of angle x, if $\overline{BC} \parallel \overline{DE}$.

A. 11°
B. 13°
C. 17°
D. 23°
E. 27°

72. How many distinct 3–digit integers can be written using only digits 0, 1, and 2, if in every integer, each digit is used only once?

F. 3
G. 4
H. 5
J. 6
K. 7

73. Find the smallest positive difference between a 3–digit number and a 2–digit number.

A. −1
B. 0
C. 1
D. 98
E. 99

74.

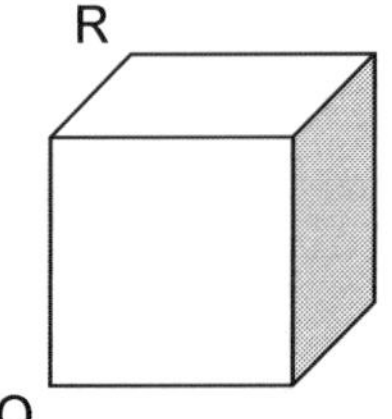

Find the perimeter of the shaded face of the cube, if $RQ = 3\sqrt{2}$ in.

F. 20 in
G. $12\sqrt{6}$ in
H. $3\sqrt{6}$ in
J. 8 in
K. 12 in

75. 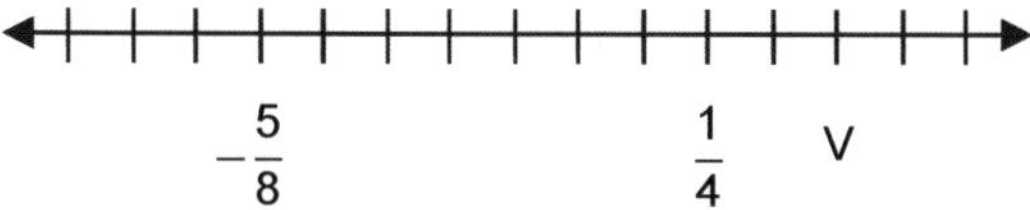

Find the coordinate of point V.

A. $\frac{5}{8}$

B. $\frac{7}{8}$

C. $\frac{1}{8}$

D. $\frac{3}{8}$

E. $\frac{1}{2}$

---

76. 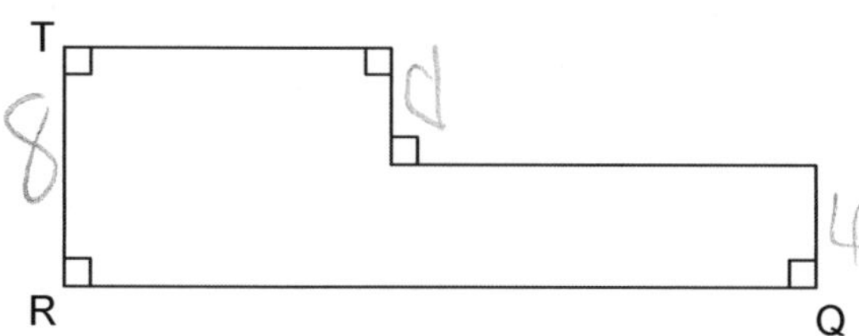

TQ (not shown) = 17 cm, TR = 8 cm. Find the perimeter of entire shape.

F. 46 cm

G. 44 cm

H. 28 cm

J. 26 cm

K. 24 cm

---

77. The ratio of a to c is 3 to 7. What is the ratio of $3c$ to $7a$?

A. 9 : 49

B. 1 : 1

C. 7 : 3

D. 1 : 2

E. Cannot be determined

---

78. If $3x - 5y + 17 = 2$, what is $5y - 3x$?

F. −19

G. 19

H. −15

J. 15

K. Cannot be determined

79.

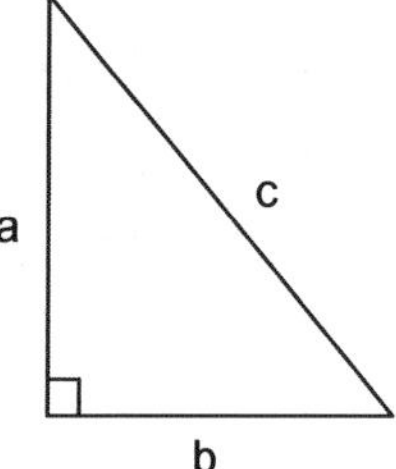

Find the value of c, if $a + b = 9$, and $ab = 16$.

A. 2
B. 4
C. 6
D. 7
E. 9

80.

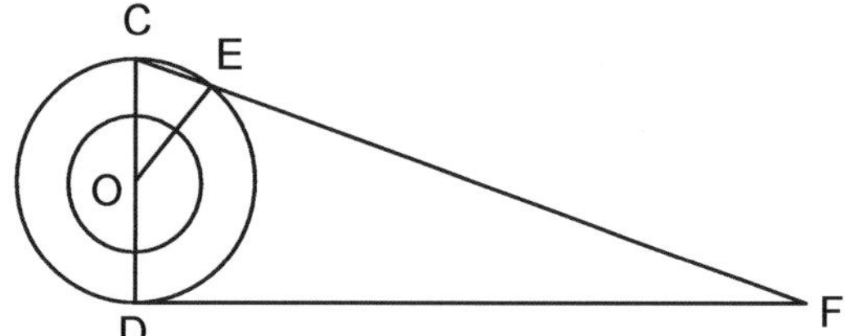

Figure is not drawn to scale.

Points C, D, and E are on the circumference of a circle. O is the center of the circle, and CD = 5. If $\angle CFD = 30°$, find perimeter of DOEF.

F. 10
G. $12.5 + 5\sqrt{3}$
H. $10 + \sqrt{3}$
J. $10 + 5\sqrt{3}$
K. 20

81. A box contains 11 pennies and 11 dimes. What is the smallest number of coins that we must remove from the box without looking to ensure that we removed more than 10 cents?

A. 11
B. 10
C. 9
D. 5
E. 1

82. The price of a jacket was increased by 20% last year, and then decreased by 20% this year. It now costs \$192. What was its original price?

F. \$200
G. \$198
H. \$208
J. \$196
K. \$192

83. Today, Sam is 3 times older than James. 11 years from today, James will be 26 years old. How old is Sam today?

A. 15
B. 19
C. 35
D. 45
E. 50

84. Two sides of an isosceles triangle are 6 cm and 12 cm. Find its perimeter.

F. 18 cm
G. 20 cm
H. 24 cm
J. 30 cm
K. 36 cm

85. If $100 - 100^c = 99.999$, find c.

A. –2
B. –1.5
C. 0
D. 1
E. 1.5

86. Steve drove for 3 hours at a speed of 60 mph, and 2 hours at a speed of 55 mph. What was his average speed for the entire trip?

F. 58 mph
G. 57.5 mph
H. 57 mph
J. 56.5 mph
K. 56 mph

87. 3, 10, 29, 66, ___, 218, 345, ...

Find the missing number in the sequence above.

A. 127
B. 129
C. 130
D. 131
E. 163

88. 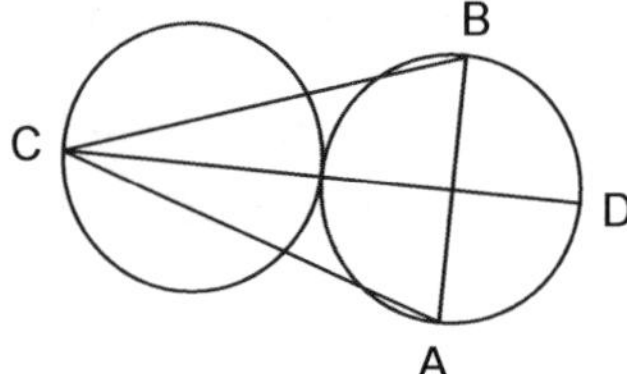

Two congruent circles with diameters 4 are tangent to each other. Line segment CD passes through the centers of both circles, and AB is the diameter of one of the circles. Find the area of triangle ABC.

F. 10
G. 12
H. 16
J. 22
K. 24

---

89. If $(x - 1)^4 = 16$, which of the following could be the value of $x - 5$?

A. -6
B. −4
C. −3
D. 3
E. 2

---

90. 10 identical machines can produce 200 items in 4 hours. How long will it take 5 of those machines to produce 300 items?

F. 14 hours
G. 12 hours
H. 10 hours
J. 8 hours
K. 6 hours

---

91. 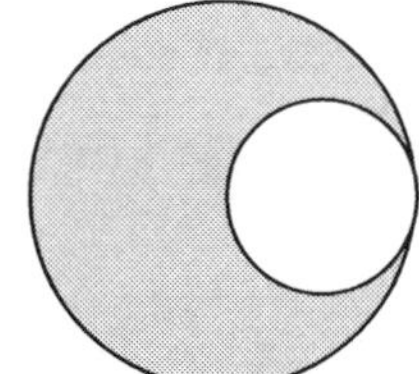

In the diagram above, the diameter of the inner circle is equal to the radius of the large circle. Two circles tangent each other. What part of the large circle is shaded?

A. $\frac{3}{4}$

B. $\frac{7}{8}$

C. $\frac{1}{8}$

D. $\frac{1}{4}$

E. $\frac{1}{3}$

92. 3, 8, 13, 18, 23, 28, 33, ...

What is the difference between the 60th and the 70th terms in the sequence above?

F. 40
G. 45
H. 50
J. 55
K. 60

93. If $-1 < x < 0$, which of the following statements are true?

I. $x < x^2$
II. $x < x^3$
III. $x^3 < x^2$

A. I only
B. II only
C. III only
D. I and III only
E. I, II, and III

94. If you write down the sequence all positive integers from 1 to 50 in a row, what is the combined number of times that digits 3 and 7 will appear in the sequence?

F. 28
G. 20
H. 18
J. 8
K. 7

95.

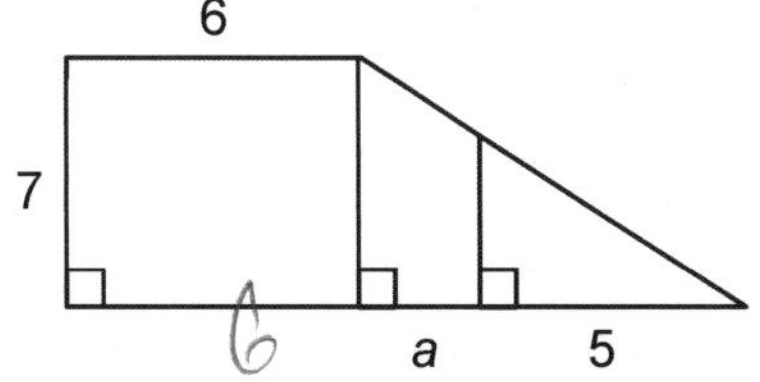

If the area of the trapezoid is 77 sq. units, then what is a?

A. 2
B. 3
C. 4
D. 5
E. 7

96. What is the largest positive difference between two 2–digit prime numbers?

F. 2
G. 17
H. 29
J. 86
K. 88

97.

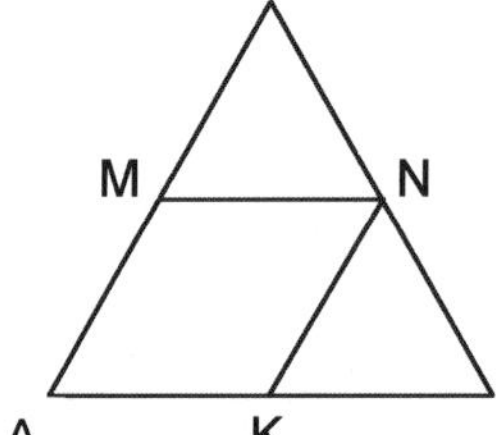

Points M, N, and K are the midpoints of the sides of a triangle. The area of the triangle is 24 cm^2. What is the area of the parallelogram AMNK?

A. 15 cm^2
B. 13 cm^2
C. 12 cm^2
D. 10 cm^2
E. 8 cm^2

98. If $11x = \sqrt{16} + \sqrt{49}$, then $x =$

F. 1
G. 2.3
H. 5.8
J. $\frac{65}{11}$
K. 6

99. If the average of 5 numbers is 6 and their product is 26, what is their sum?

A. 30
B. 27
C. 26
D. 18
E. 14

100. The sum of two consecutive integers is t. In terms of t, what is the sum of the next two consecutive integers?

F. 5t + 4
G. 4t + 4
H. 3t + 4
J. 2t + 4
K. t + 4

SHSAT Practice Math Test 8

SHSAT PRACTICE TEST 8

PART 2 — MATHEMATICS

Suggested Time — 75 Minutes

50 QUESTIONS

---

51. If $27 - x = 18 - y$, what is $x - y$?

A. 43
B. 11
C. 9
D. –9
E. –43

---

52. $(\sqrt{9} + \sqrt{36})^2 =$

F. 180
G. 81
H. 45
J. 29
K. 27

---

53. If the Greatest Common Factor of 24 and P is 8, what is a possible value of P?

A. 10
B. 12
C. 16
D. 36
E. 42

54. One side of a triangle is 4 cm, the sum of two other sides is 11 cm, and all sides are integers. What is the largest possible side of the triangle?

F. 9 cm
G. 8 cm
H. 7 cm
J. 6 cm
K. 5 cm

---

55. The operation ۞ is defined for all nonzero numbers by k ۞ $t = -k^2 - t$. Find (5 ۞ –24) ۞ 2.

A. 2399
B. 79
C. 0
D. –2
E. –3

56. If the temperature at 6 AM was 18°F, and 6 hours later it dropped to 18° below zero, what was the temperature's rate of change?

- **F.** 6° per hour
- **G.** 5° per hour
- **H.** 4° per hour
- **J.** 3° per hour
- **K.** 8° per hour

57. How many integers are in the interval between –7 and 1.9?

- **A.** 2
- **B.** 3
- **C.** 7
- **D.** 8
- **E.** Infinitely many

58. What is 20% of $\frac{3}{8}$ of 240?

- **F.** 8
- **G.** 18
- **H.** 20
- **J.** 24
- **K.** None of these

59. If $(2x - 3) \div x = x + 5$, what is the value of $x^2 + 3x + 3$?

- **A.** –3
- **B.** –2
- **C.** –1
- **D.** 0
- **E.** 17

60. If p is a positive integer, then $2p(2p + 1)(2p - 1)$ is always divisible by

- **F.** 8
- **G.** 7
- **H.** 6
- **J.** 5
- **K.** 4

61. If $h < 20$ and $h - 5g = 0$, which of the following must be true?

- **A.** $g > 4$
- **B.** $g > 100$
- **C.** $g < 4$
- **D.** $g < 80$
- **E.** $g < 100$

62.

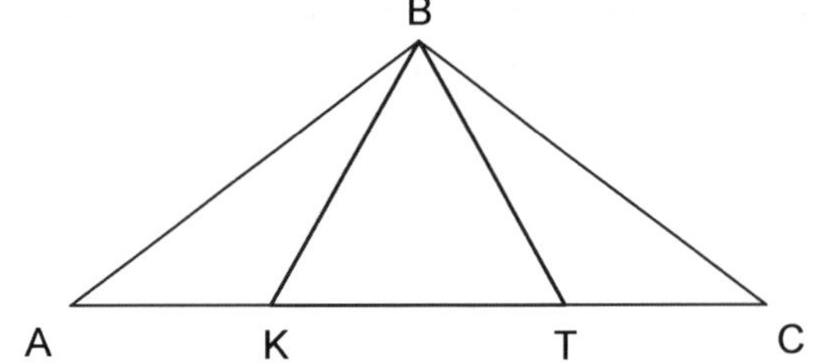

Triangle KBT is equilateral, AB = BC, and AK = CT. If ∠KAB = 15°, find the degree measure of angle ABK.

F. 35°

G. 36°

H. 38°

J. 40°

K. 45°

63. If $A = 3B = 0.25C = 0.1D = E > 0$, which of the variables is the greatest?

A. A

B. B

C. C

D. D

E. E

64. Rectangle (not shown) has a length of 11 cm and a width of 5 cm. If 1 cm^2 squares are cut out of each corner of the rectangle, what is the perimeter of the new figure?

F. 24 cm

G. 28 cm

H. 30 cm

J. 32 cm

K. 36 cm

65. How many prime numbers are divisible by 17?

A. None

B. 5

C. 3

D. 2

E. 1

66. 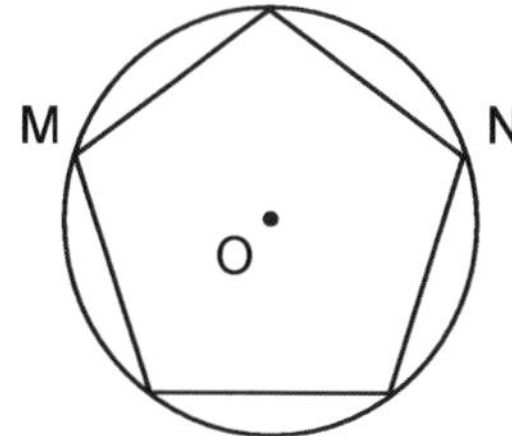

Regular pentagon is inscribed into a circle. If O is the center of the circle, Find the degree measure of the angle MON.

F. 288°
G. 150°
H. 144°
J. 130°
K. 120°

---

67. If a 20% deposit that has been paid toward the purchase of a sofa is $120, how much more remains to be paid?

A. $480
B. $360
C. $240
D. $120
E. $30

---

68. How many integers g will satisfy the inequality $7 < 3g - 1 \leq 17$?

F. 1
G. 2
H. 3
J. 4
K. 5

---

69. ⊕ ⊖ ⊗ ⊘ ⊙ ⊚ ⊛ ⊜ ⊖ ⊕ ⊖ ⊗ ⊘ ⊙ ⊚ ⊛ ⊜ ⊖ …

Which shape will be at the 111th position in the pattern above?

A. ⊕
B. ⊖
C. ⊗
D. ⊘
E. ⊛

---

70. ⑥ ⓫ ⑧ ⓭ ⑪ ⓯ ⓿ ❹ ⑮ ❷

If a marble is randomly chosen from the set shown above, what is the probability of choosing a black marble with an even number?

F. 0.5
G. 0.4
H. 0.3
J. 0.2
K. 0.1

71. The average of 3 numbers from a set of six numbers is 7, and the average of 3 other numbers from the same set is 11. What is the average of all 6 numbers?

A. 18
B. 12
C. 11
D. 9
E. 8

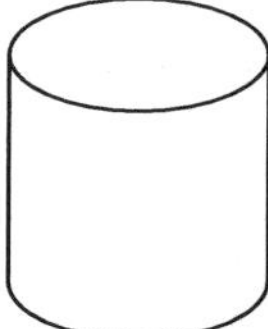

Find the longest distance between a point on the top circumference and a point on the base circumference of the cylinder, if the radius of the base is 4 and the height of the cylinder is 6.

F. 10
G. 9
H. 8
J. 6
K. 5

73. The sum of p consecutive integers is 3. What can p be?

A. 9
B. 8
C. 7
D. 6
E. 5

74. A bus travels the first 130 miles in 2 hours, and the second 200 miles at the rate of 50 mph. What was the average speed of the bus for the entire trip?

F. 67.5 mph
G. 60 mph
H. 58 mph
J. 57.5 mph
K. 55 mph

75. The ratio of k to q is 7 to 9. What is the ratio of $7q$ to the $3k$?

A. 49 : 27
B. 7 : 9
C. 9 : 7
D. 3 : 1
E. Cannot be determined

76. If 40 is 40% of 40% of an integer, what is the integer?

F. 20
G. 50
H. 250
J. 500
K. 1000

77. 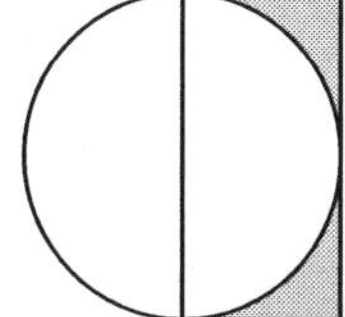

If the diameter of the circle in the diagram above is 2, what is the area of the shaded part of the rectangle?

A. $2 - \pi$
B. $20 - \pi$
C. $2 - 0.5\pi$
D. $20 - 0.5\pi$
E. $200 - \pi$

78. Find x, if $(a + a)^2 = 4a^{5 - 3x}$.

F. 0
G. 1
H. 2
J. 3
K. 4

79. A box contains 7 red balls and 2 blue balls. How many more blue balls you need to add to the box to make the probability of randomly picking a red ball equal to 0.5?

A. 2
B. 3
C. 4
D. 5
E. None of these

80. If $1 - 0.999 = 10^{-3n}$, what is n?

F. -1
G. -3
H. 1
J. 2
K. None of these

81. How many multiples of 5 are there between 12 and 77?

A. 12
B. 13
C. 14
D. 17
E. 19

82. Which number is the reciprocal of 2.5?

F. 4
G. –0.4
H. 10.4
J. –2.5
K. 0.4

83. C and B are both two–digit positive integers. The tens digit of C is less than 6, and the ones digit of B is greater than 5. What is the largest possible difference $C - B$?

A. 49
B. 43
C. 40
D. 39
E. 37

84.

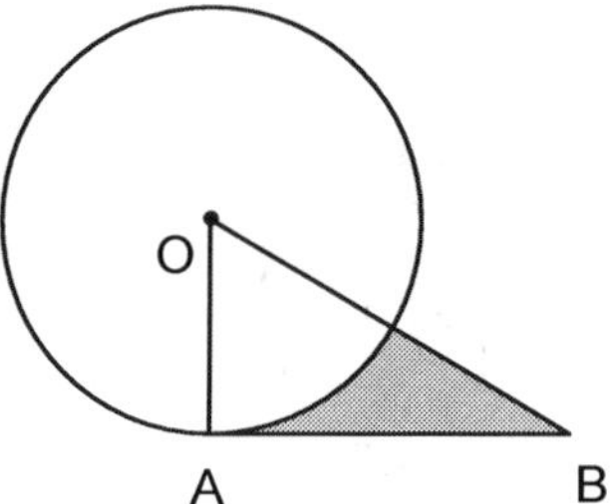

AB is tangent to circle O with radius 6, and ∠ABO = 30°. Find the area of the shaded region.

F. $18\sqrt{3} - 6\pi$
G. $18 - 6\pi$
H. $36\sqrt{3} - 6\pi$
J. $6\sqrt{3} - 6\pi$
K. $9\sqrt{3} - 6\pi$

85. A package of postcards costs \$40. Each individual postcard costs \$0.85. What is the greatest number of individual postcards that you can buy so that the total price is smaller than that of a package?

A. 50
B. 49
C. 48
D. 47
E. 46

86.

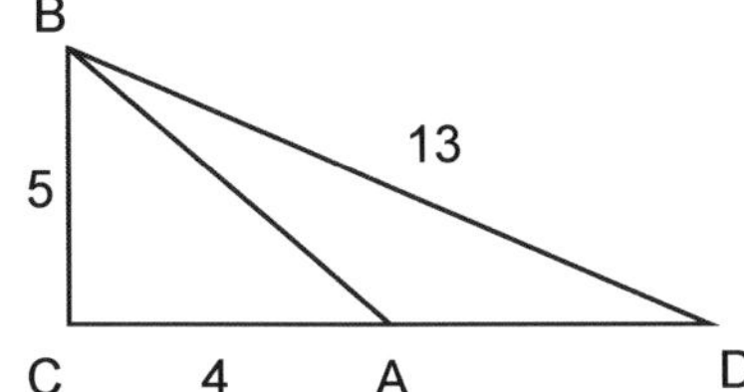

DBC is a right triangle, and point A lies on the line segment CD. Find AD.

F. 10
G. 9
H. 8
J. 7
K. 6

---

87. A car made a 60 mile trip at an average speed of 20 mph. On the return trip, the car's average speed was 30 mph. What was the average speed of the car for the entire two–way trip?

A. 30 mph
B. 26.5 mph
C. 26 mph
D. 24.5 mph
E. 24 mph

---

88. 4, 7, 10, 13, 16, 19, ...

What is the 100th term of the sequence above?

F. 301
G. 300
H. 297
J. 294
K. 291

89.

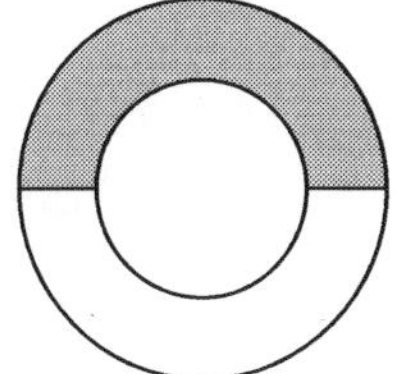

In the diagram above, the radius of the outer circle is 10, and the width of the space between the circles is 4. Find the area of the shaded part of the figure.

A. 40π
B. 36π
C. 32π
D. 28π
E. 24π

90. The average of six consecutive integers is 12.5. What is the average of the next six consecutive integers?

F. 18
G. 18.5
H. 19
J. 19.5
K. 20

91.

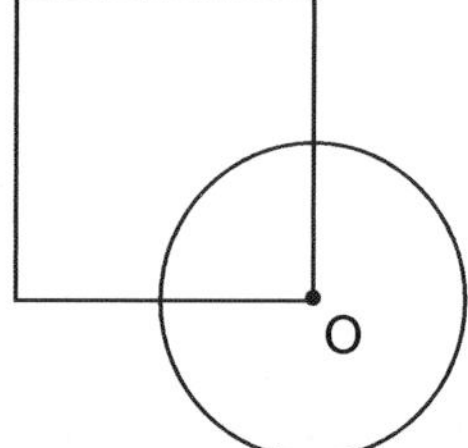

A circle and a square overlap as shown in the diagram, with the center of the circle and the corner of the square lying at point O. If the area of the square is 16, and the radius of the circle is 2, what is the total area of the figure?

A. $16 + 3\pi$
B. $16 - 3\pi$
C. $12 + 3\pi$
D. $12 - 3\pi$
E. $10 + 3\pi$

92. Square Q has an area of 25 in^2. Square P has a perimeter 4 inches less than square Q. What is the area of square P?

F. 25 in^2
G. 20 in^2
H. 16 in^2
J. 12 in^2
K. 8 in^2

93. What is the area of the triangle with vertices (2,7), (8,7), and (20,9)?

A. 6 sq. units
B. 8 sq. units
C. 12 sq. units
D. 15 sq. units
E. 16 sq. units

94. 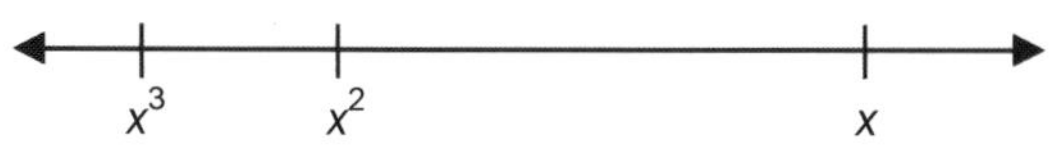

If x, x^2, and x^3 lie on the number line in the given order, which number could be the value of x?

F. -2

G. $-\frac{1}{2}$

H. $\frac{3}{8}$

J. 1

K. 1.5

95. 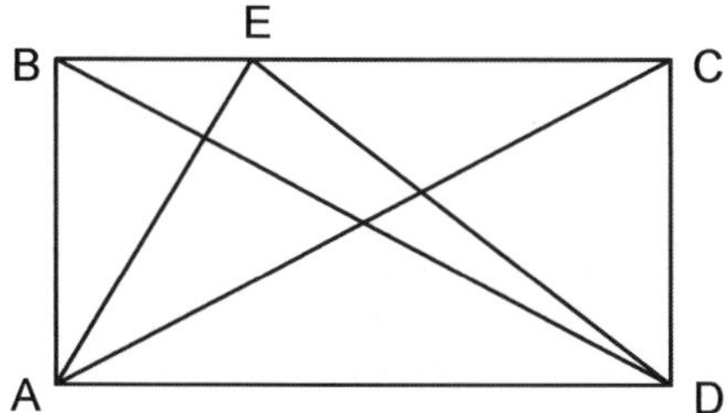

In the diagram above, all triangles whose vertices lie on the perimeter of rectangle ABCD have the same area, **except**

A. $\triangle$AEC

B. $\triangle$ABC

C. $\triangle$ACD

D. $\triangle$AED

E. $\triangle$BCD

96. There are twice as many students in grade 8A than in grade 8B. The average score on the math test in 8A is 90, and in 8B it's 87. What is the average math test score of all students in grade 8A and 8B?

F. 90

G. 89

H. 88

J. 87.5

K. 87

97. Nick has 32 nickels and quarters. The total value of Nick's coins is $4.60. How many nickels does he have?

A. 15

B. 16

C. 17

D. 18

E. 20

98. 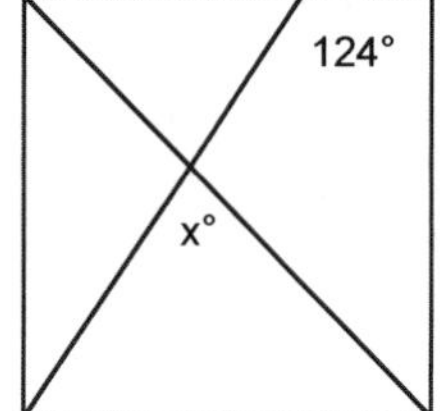

Find the angle of intersection of the diagonal of the square and the line which forms the angle of 124° with the top side of the square, as shown in the diagram above.

F. 76°
G. 79°
H. 80°
J. 82°
K. 86°

99. A group of 3 workers needs 20 days to do a certain job. How long would it take a group of 4 workers to do the same job, if each worker performs at the same rate?

A. 24
B. 20
C. 18
D. 15
E. 12

100. 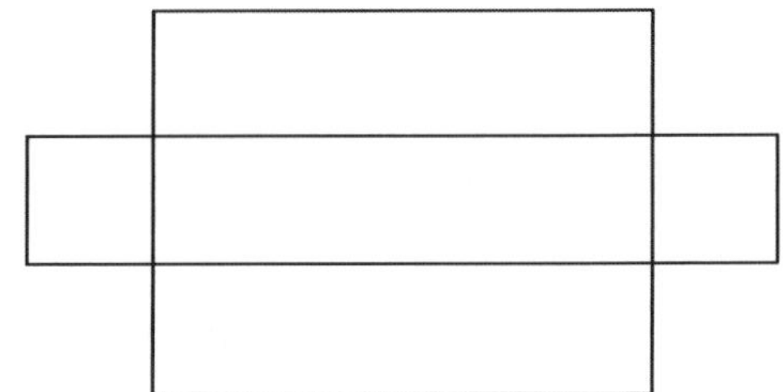

Two rectangles with dimensions of 2 by 12 and 6 by 8 overlap each other as shown and have two common lines of symmetry. The longest side of each rectangle is horizontal. Find the perimeter of the entire figure.

F. 54
G. 50
H. 48
J. 46
K. 36

SHSAT Practice Math Test 9

SHSAT PRACTICE TEST 9

PART 2 — MATHEMATICS

Suggested Time — 75 Minutes

50 QUESTIONS

51. If $3m(2 - 12) - 2m(3 + 12) = 0$, find the value of m.

A. -1
B. 0
C. 1
D. -2
E. 2

52. If the circumference of a circle is 1, find a central angle corresponding to its arc that is $\frac{2}{5}$ long.

F. 144°
G. 108°
H. 72°
J. 36°
K. 24°

53. 2 oranges cost as much as 3 pears. 1 pear costs as much as 5 onions. How many onions cost as much as 4 oranges?

A. 6
B. 12
C. 15
D. 30
E. 32

54. If the side of a square is as long as the diameter of a circle, find the ratio of the perimeter of the square to the circumference of the circle.

F. $4 : 1$
G. $1 : 4$
H. $\pi : 1$
J. $1 : \pi$
K. $4 : \pi$

55. In the sequence, $1^1, 2^4, 3^9, 4^{16}, \ldots, 9^n$ find the value of n.

A. 625
B. 169
C. 121
D. 81
E. 49

56. Two cars are 300 miles apart and moving towards each other at 36 mph and 24 mph, respectively. If they started driving at 1 PM, at what time will they meet each other?

F. 6:00 PM
G. 5:00 PM
H. 4:00 PM
J. 5:00 AM
K. 6:00 AM

57. 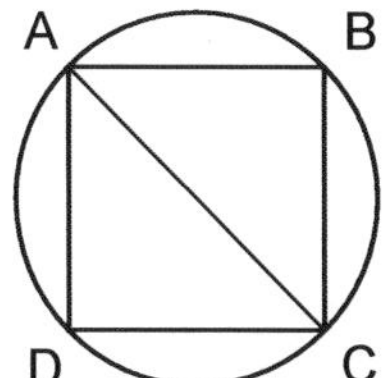

A square is inscribed in a circle, as shown. If the diagonal of the square is 36, find the circumference of the circle.

A. 12π
B. 18π
C. 24π
D. 36π
E. 48π

58. If $m = 0.2n$ and $n = 2.5k$, then what part of k is m?

F. 0.5
G. 0.05
H. 0.4
J. 0.3
K. None of these

59. If $16^2 = 8^{3-x}$, find x.

A. –3

B. –2

C. 1

D. $\frac{1}{2}$

E. $\frac{1}{3}$

60. If t students in the class like the blue color, k students in the class like the red color, and p students in the class like both blue and red colors, how many students are in the class, if $t + k - p = 24$?

F. 26

G. 24

H. 22

J. 20

K. cannot be determined

61.

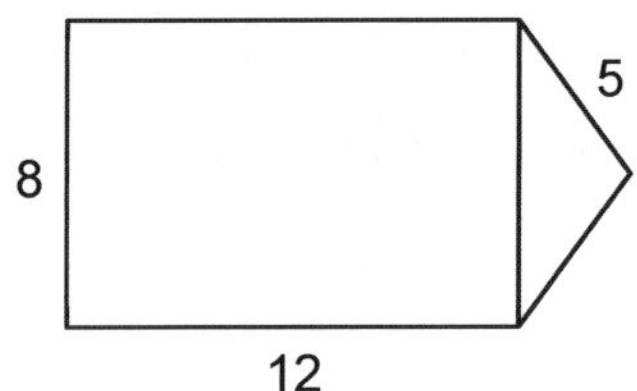

An isosceles triangle shares a side with a rectangle, as shown above. What is the area of the entire figure?

A. 100

B. 102

C. 104

D. 108

E. 116

62.

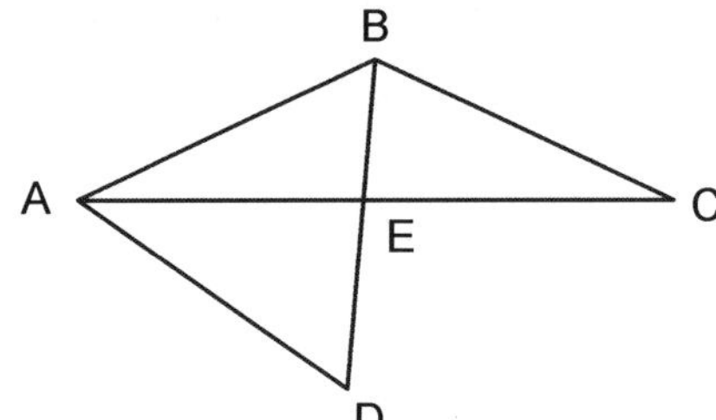

Triangle ABD is equilateral and triangle ABC is isosceles. If $\angle BCA = 25°$, find the degree measure of angle BEC.

F. 85°

G. 80°

H. 75°

J. 70°

K. 65°

63. If $v > t$, $q < v$, $q > p$, $t < p$, which of the variables is the largest?

A. v
B. q
C. t
D. p
E. cannot be determined

64.

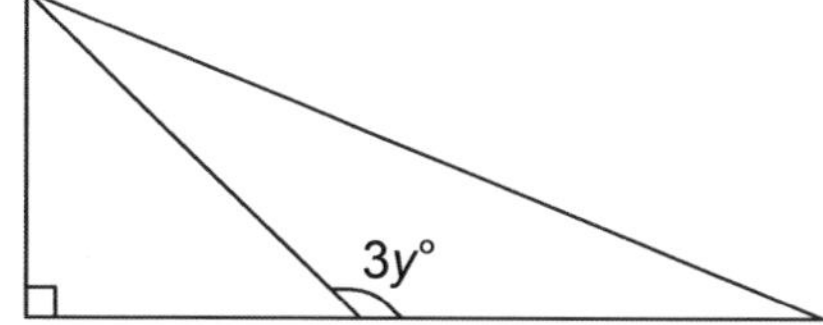

In the diagram above, which of the following could be a value of y?

F. 20°
G. 30°
H. 35°
J. 60°
K. 65°

65. How many prime numbers are sums of two odd integers?

A. None
B. 1
C. 2
D. 3
E. more than 3

66.

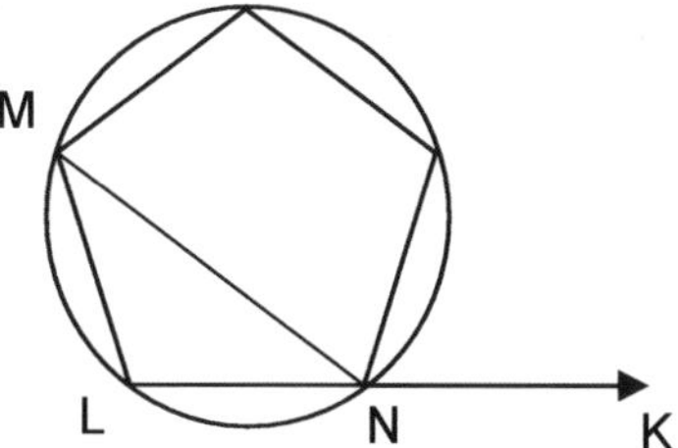

A regular pentagon is inscribed into a circle. Find the degree measure of the angle MNK.

F. 288°
G. 150°
H. 144°
J. 130°
K. 120°

67. If $a\%$ of b is divided by $b\%$ of a and the quotient is multiplied by 5, the result will be:

A. 500
B. 50
C. 5
D. 1
E. 0

68. How many integers g will satisfy the inequality $8 \le |3g - 1| \le 11$?

F. 1
G. 2
H. 3
J. 4
K. 5

69.

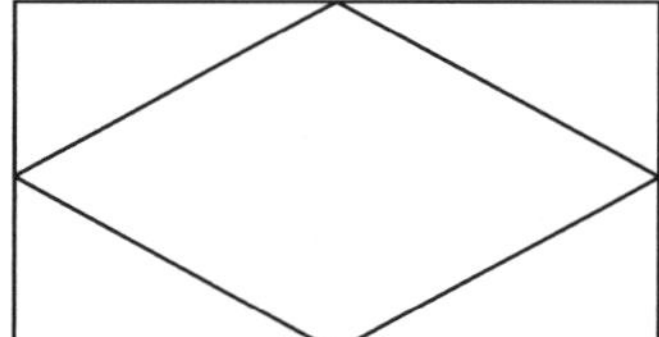

In the diagram above, if the side of the interior rhombus is 13 cm and the length of its shorter diagonal is 10 cm, what is the area of the outer rectangle?

A. 240 cm^2
B. 120 cm^2
C. 116 cm^2
D. 112 cm^2
E. 60 cm^2

70. ⑥ ⓫ ⓭ ⑪ ⓯ ⓿ ❹ ⑮ ❷ ① ⑲ ⑤

If a marble is chosen randomly from the set above, what is the probability that it's a white marble with a prime number on it?

F. $\frac{1}{12}$
G. $\frac{1}{6}$
H. $\frac{1}{4}$
J. $\frac{1}{2}$
K. $\frac{7}{12}$

71. The average of five distinct positive integers is 20, and the median is 12. What is the largest possible number in this set?

A. 74
B. 72
C. 64
D. 62
E. 52

72. Two sides of a triangle are 7 and 8. What is the largest possible perimeter of the triangle, if the third side is also an integer?

F. 30
G. 29
H. 28
J. 16
K. 15

73. $4^{17} + 4^{17} + 4^{17} + 4^{17} =$

A. 4^{17}
B. 2^{36}
C. 16^{17}
D. 4^{4}
E. 4^{68}

74. Simplify:
$3(a - 5) - 2(1 - 4a) - (11a + 6) =$

F. -23
G. -11
H. $-16a - 23$
J. 13
K. $19 - 16a$

75. The ratio of p to q is 2 to 3. What is the ratio of q^2 to the $3p^2$?

A. 9 : 16
B. 4 : 3
C. 3 : 4
D. 16 : 9
E. Cannot be determined

76. A 300 ounce mixture is 12% acid. If 100 ounces of water evaporated, what percent of the new mixture is acid?

F. 12%
G. 18%
H. 20%
J. 36%
K. 72%

77. 

Two identical cubes share a face as shown in the diagram above. If the side of each cube is 4, find the distance HE.

A. 16
B. $8\sqrt{6}$
C. $4\sqrt{6}$
D. $2\sqrt{6}$
E. 6

78. If x and y are two different integers, and $x^2 = 4$, and $y^2 = 49$, what is the largest possible value for $y - x$?

F. 5
G. 6
H. 7
J. 8
K. 9

79. 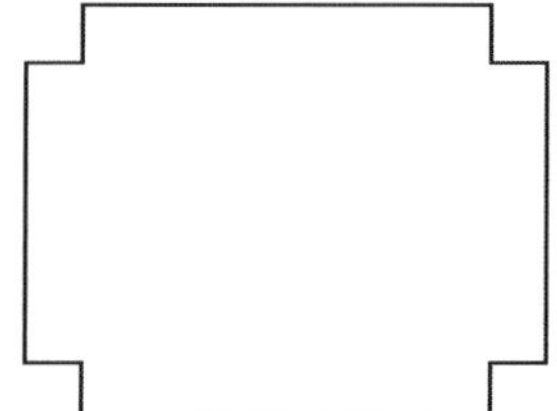

Sam used a piece of cardboard to make a box by cutting equal squares from each corner of the board, as shown above, and folding up the sides. All three dimensions of the box are distinct integers and the volume is 35 in^3. Find the perimeter of the original piece of cardboard.

A. 46 in
B. 42 in
C. 32 in
D. 28 in
E. 24 in

80. 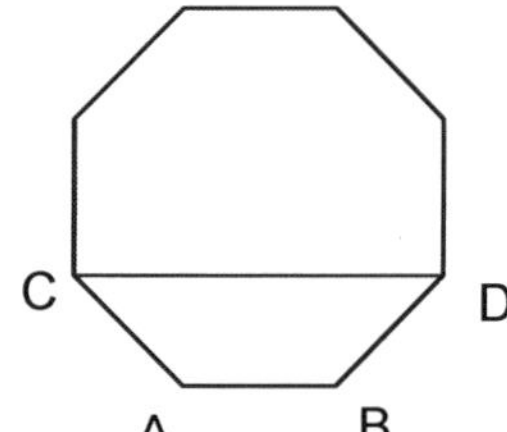

If each side of the regular octagon is 2, what is the length of CD?

F. $2\sqrt{2} + 2$
G. $4\sqrt{2}$
H. $\sqrt{2} + 2$
J. 4
K. 2

81.

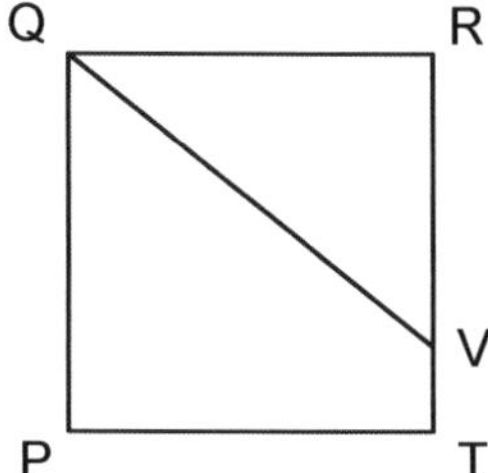

The perimeter of the square PQRT is 4. The length of QV could be:

A. 2
B. 1.7
C. 1.5
D. 1.3
E. 1

82. If $a + b = 29$, $b + c = 37$, and $a + c = 42$, what is the average of a, b, and c?

F. 18
G. 19
H. 36
J. 54
K. 108

83. If the product of two numbers is 23 and the sum of their reciprocals is 2, what is the sum of these numbers?

A. 14
B. 18.5
C. 23
D. 23.5
E. 46

84.

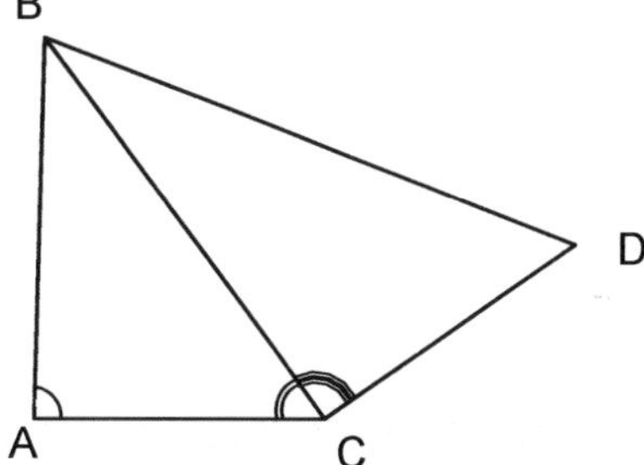

If $\angle BAC = 88°$, $\angle BCA = 53°$, and $\angle BCD = 93°$, which line segment is the longest?

F. AB
G. BC
H. CD
J. AC
K. BD

85. If p and q are integers, how many distinct ordered pairs (p, q) satisfy the equation $4p + 6q = 13$?

A. 4
B. 3
C. 2
D. 1
E. None

86. If $-2 < x < 6$, and x is an integer, what is the smallest possible value of $x^2 - 3$?

F. -4
G. -3
H. -2
J. -1
K. 0

87.

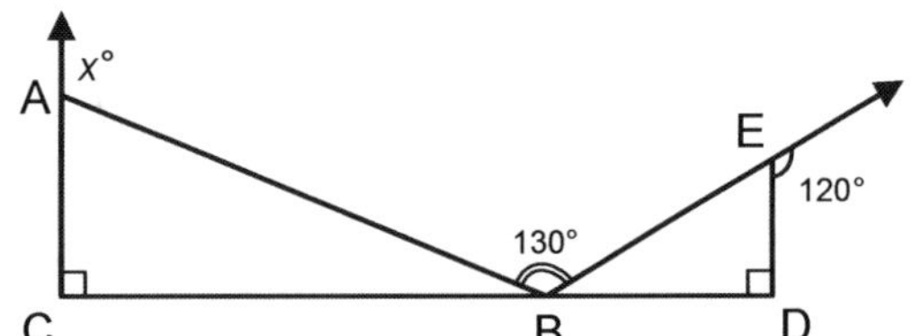

Find x.

A. 110°
B. 120°
C. 130°
D. 140°
E. 150°

88. 0, 1, 4, 9, 16, 25, 36, ...

What is the 15th term of the sequence above?

F. 256
G. 225
H. 196
J. 169
K. 144

89.

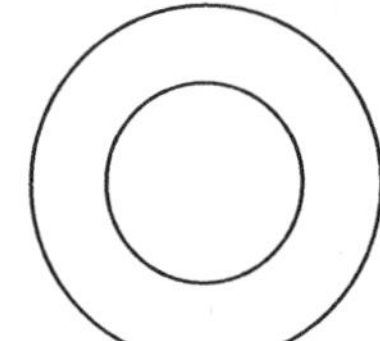

In the diagram above, the area of the inner circle is 25% of the area of the outer circle. What is the ratio of the radius of the outer circle to the radius of the inner circle?

A. 1 : 2
B. 1 : 3
C. 2 : 1
D. 2 : 3
E. 1 : 4

90. Which of the following is not $\frac{1}{3}$ of an integer?

F. -7

G. $-\frac{1}{3}$

H. 1

J. $\frac{1}{3}$

K. $\frac{1}{2}$

91. 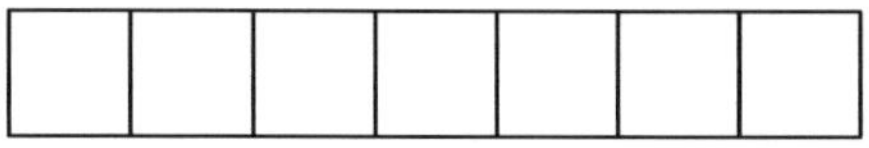

A rectangle consists of 7 congruent squares, as shown above. If the perimeter of the rectangle is 96 cm, what is the area of each square?

A. 16 cm^2

B. 25 cm^2

C. 36 cm^2

D. 47 cm^2

E. 64 cm^2

92. Ann is 24 years older than Denny. In 10 years, Ann will be 3 times as old as Denny. How old is Ann now?

F. 25

G. 26

H. 27

J. 28

K. 29

93. What is the area of the triangle that the line $y = 2 - x$, the x–axis, and the y–axis form in the first quadrant?

A. 1 sq. unit

B. 2 sq. units

C. 3 sq. units

D. 4 sq. units

E. 6 sq. units

94. 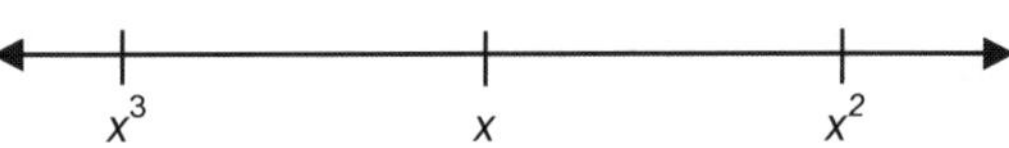

If x, x^2, and x^3 lie on the number line in the given order, what could be the value of x?

F. -2

G. $-\frac{1}{2}$

H. $\frac{3}{8}$

J. 1

K. 1.5

95. If the average of $(2a + b)$, $(3a - 2b)$, and $(4a + b)$ is 12, what is a?

A. 12
B. 6
C. 4
D. 3
E. 2

96. If $y^2 - 5x^2 = 11$, and x and y are positive integers, what could be the value of y?

F. 5
G. 4
H. 3
J. 2
K. 1

97. The sum of two numbers is 26, and their positive difference is 12. Find the larger number.

A. 21
B. 19
C. 17
D. 15
E. 7

98. All dimensions of a box are integers. The areas of 3 different faces are 15 in^2, 21 in^2, and 35 in^2, respectively. Find the volume of the box.

F. 30 in^3
G. 90 in^3
H. 96 in^3
J. 105 in^3
K. 115 in^3

99. Jim can paint the wall in 6 hours; John can paint the same wall in 12 hours. How long will it take them to do the job together?

A. 6 hours
B. 5 hours
C. 4 hours
D. 3 hours
E. 2 hours

100.

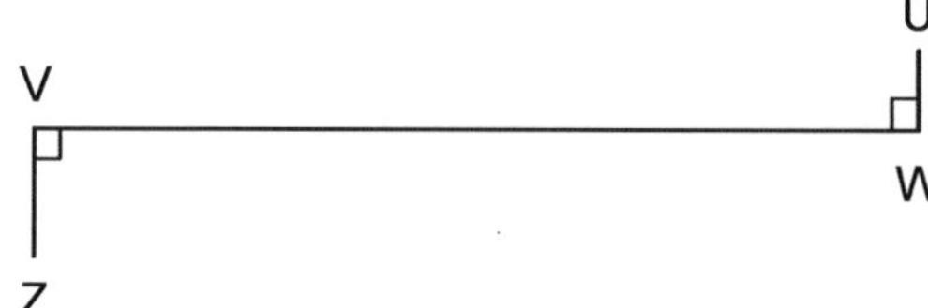

If ZV = 6, VW = 24, and WU = 4, how long is the distance ZU (not shown)?

F. 26
G. 25
H. 24
J. 23
K. 22

SHSAT Practice Math Test 10

SHSAT PRACTICE TEST 10

PART 2 — MATHEMATICS

Suggested Time — 75 Minutes

50 QUESTIONS

---

51. What is the product of the smallest prime number and the largest negative integer?

A. –2
B. –1
C. 0
D. 1
E. Negative infinity

---

52. How many even integers are there between –7 and 7?

F. 11
G. 10
H. 8
J. 7
K. 6

53. Jane has read 108 pages from a book. Kevin is reading the same book, and has 80 pages left to read. If there are 200 pages in the book, by how many percent is the number of pages left for Jane greater than for Kevin?

A. 58%
B. 60%
C. 25%
D. 20%
E. 15%

---

54. The operation ◗◖ is defined for all nonzero numbers by ◗X◖ = 3X – 1. Find ◗5◖ + ◗–7◖ .

F. –8
G. –7
H. –6
J. 6
K. –36

55. 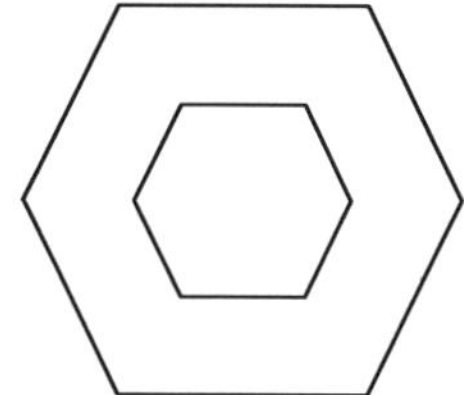

Two similar regular hexagons have a common center. If each side of the big hexagon is twice the side of the small one and the area of the small hexagon is 3 sq. in, what is the area of the big hexagon?

A. 6 sq. in.
B. 9 sq. in.
C. 12 sq. in.
D. 16 sq. in.
E. 24 sq. in.

56. $\sqrt{169} - \sqrt{144} = \sqrt{N}$. Find N.

F. 1
G. 2
H. 5
J. 12.5
K. 25

57. Round 98.9998 to the nearest thousandths.

A. 99.000
B. 98.900
C. 98.990
D. 99.990
E. 100

58. There are 20 lab mice in a cage. For every 3 gray mice, there is 1 white mouse. How many gray mice are there?

F. 3
G. 6
H. 9
J. 15
K. 19

59. Solve the equation for x:
$3 + (1 \div x) = 2$

A. −2
B. −1
C. 0
D. 1
E. 2

60. What is the smallest 3–digit number that is divisible by 3, but not divisible by 6?

F. 102
G. 103
H. 105
J. 109
K. 111

61. If $a(a - b) = 117$ and $ab = 52$, what is a?

A. 13
B. 11
C. 9
D. 7
E. 4

62. $(29.8)(17.9) - (29.8)(7.9) =$

F. 29
G. 298
H. 289
J. 28.9
K. None of these

63. There are a few red marbles and a few green marbles in the bag. If the ratio of the number of red marbles to the number of green marbles is 7 : 8, what could be the total number of marbles in the bag?

A. 12
B. 13
C. 19
D. 23
E. 30

64. The sum of 7 consecutive odd numbers is 91. What is the sum of the two largest numbers in this set?

F. 36
G. 35
H. 34
J. 33
K. 32

65. The product of 8 numbers is negative. At most how many of these 8 numbers are negative?

A. 8
B. 7
C. 6
D. 5
E. 1

66. What is the largest possible value of y, if $y = -|3 - x| + 5$?

F. 3
G. 5
H. 8
J. 11
K. 17

67. If $A > B$, $C < A$, $D < B$, and $E = D$, the largest number is:

A. A
B. B
C. C
D. D
E. Cannot be determined

68. 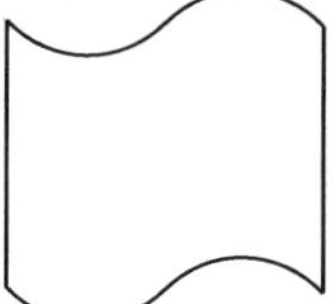

How many lines of symmetry does the figure above have?

F. 0
G. 1
H. 2
J. 3
K. 4

69. Kevin got 80% on the test, and Eli got a 96%. By what percent is Eli's score higher than Kevin's score?

A. 10%
B. 16%
C. 20%
D. 25%
E. 26%

70. For the set of integers {2, 3, 7, X, 9}, find X if 7 is the median of the set.

F. 7
G. 8
H. 9
J. 10
K. Cannot be determined

71. If the area of a square is numerically twice the perimeter of that square, what is the side of the square?

A. 8
B. 7
C. 6
D. 5
E. 1

72. Danny has only quarters and pennies in his piggy bank. The number of quarters is the same as the number of pennies. Which of the following amounts is a possible total of the money in the piggy bank?

F. \$1.17
G. \$2.25
H. \$4.80
J. \$7.80
K. \$8.70

73.

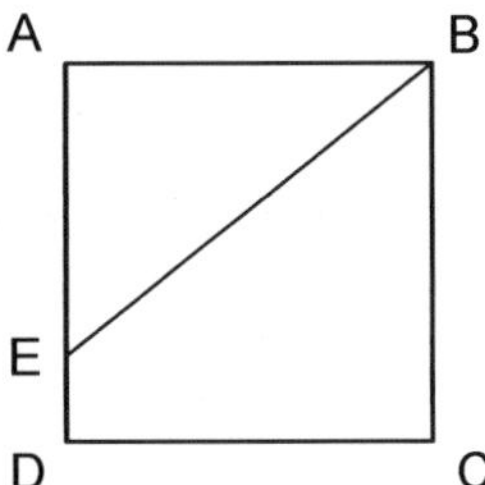

ABCD is a square with area 16 cm^2. If DE is one–fourth of AD, what is the area of DEBC?

A. 12 cm^2
B. 11 cm^2
C. 10 cm^2
D. 8 cm^2
E. 4 cm^2

74. If some proper fraction and its reciprocal are added together, the result is 2.9. What is the fraction?

F. $\frac{1}{2}$
G. $\frac{1}{3}$
H. $\frac{2}{3}$
J. $\frac{2}{5}$
K. $\frac{2}{7}$

75. 12112111211112...

If the pattern above is continued, what will be the sum of all digits from 40th to 44th position?

A. 7
B. 6
C. 5
D. 4
E. 3

76. Find the average of $2b$, $5b$, $7b$, and $10b$.

F. $2b$
G. $6b$
H. $2b + 1$
J. $2b - 1$
K. $12b$

77.

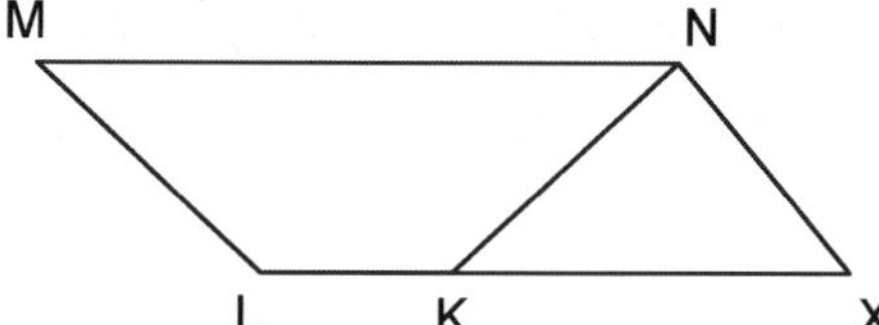

KLMN is an isosceles trapezoid with LM = KN and ∠M = 42°. If the measure of ∠KNX of the triangle KNX is 88°, find the measure of angle X.

A. 36°
B. 44°
C. 50°
D. 56°
E. 62°

78. What is the smallest integer that can be added to 109,456 to make the result divisible by 7?

F. 2
G. 3
H. 4
J. 5
K. 6

79. Security checkpoint A checks every 3rd piece of luggage, and security checkpoint B checks every 4th piece of luggage. How many pieces of luggage in a batch of 200 will be checked twice?

A. 20
B. 18
C. 17
D. 16
E. 15

---

80. If $2x^2 - 3x = 5$, what is $4x^2 - 6x + 1$?

F. 11
G. 12
H. 26
J. 27
K. None of these

---

81. Find the area of the triangle ABC, if A(−1, 3), B(2, 3), and C(4, 5).

A. 2 units^2
B. 3 units^2
C. 4 units^2
D. 6 units^2
E. 6.25 units^2

---

82. Express C in terms of X and Y, if $Y = 2C - 3X$.

F. $C = 0.5(3X + Y)$
G. $C = 1 - 3X$
H. $C = 0.5(3X - Y)$
J. $C = 3X + Y$
K. $C = 2Y - 3X$

---

83. The average of 4 different positive integers is 11. What is the greatest possible value one of these integers could have?

A. 44
B. 41
C. 39
D. 38
E. 36

84.

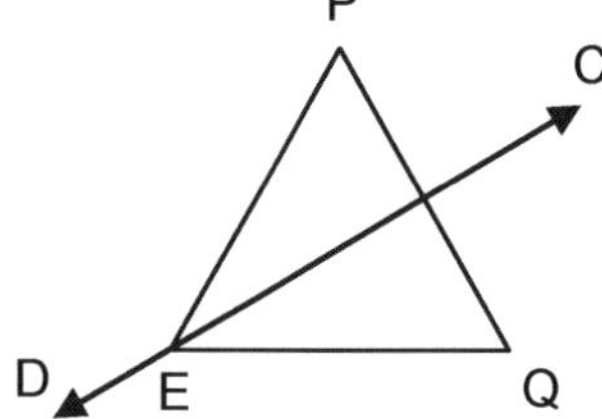

Line CD forms a right angle with the side PQ of the equilateral triangle EPQ. Find the measure of the angle DEP.

F. 160°
G. 150°
H. 130°
J. 120°
K. 110°

85. There are 25 color chips in the box. The probability of picking a red chip is 0.2. How many red chips must be added to increase the probability of getting red to 0.5?

A. 20
B. 15
C. 10
D. 8
E. 6

86.

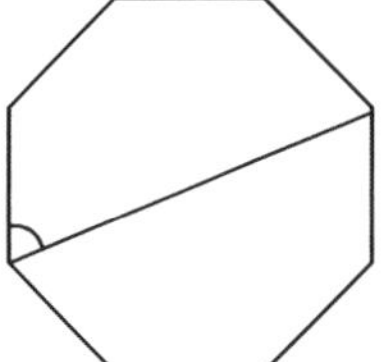

What is the degree measure of the angle between the longest diagonal of a regular octagon and its side?

F. 67.5°
G. 68°
H. 68.5°
J. 70°
K. 75°

87. If $-6 \leq x \leq -4$ and $4 \leq y \leq 6$, what is the smallest possible value of xy?

A. 0
B. –6
C. –16
D. –24
E. –36

88. What is the largest integer d that will satisfy the inequality: $3d - 5 < 7$?

F. –2
G. –1
H. 0
J. 3
K. Cannot be determined

89. What is the radius of the circle whose area is numerically 5 times greater than its circumference?

A. 5
B. 10
C. 4π
D. 2π
E. π

90. During the first 120 miles of a 240 mile journey, a truck driver maintained an average speed of 50 mph. What was his average speed during the next 120 miles, if the average speed of the entire trip was 60 mph?

F. 75 mph
G. 72 mph
H. 70 mph
J. 68 mph
K. 64 mph

91.

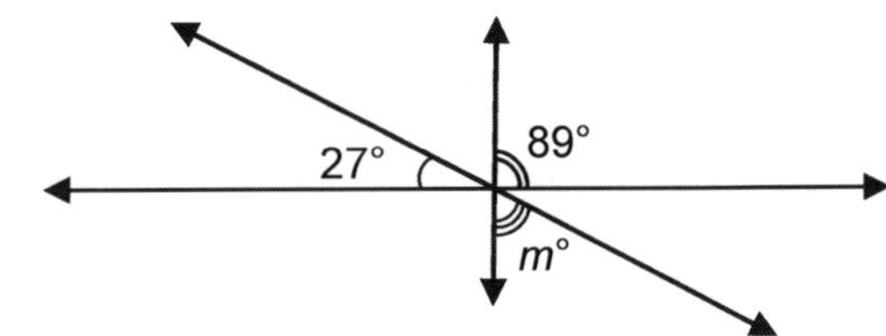

Find the measure of angle $m°$.

A. 55°
B. 54°
C. 67°
D. 65°
E. 64°

92. Two infinite sets M = {5, 10, 15, 20, 25, …}; and N = {7, 14, 21, 28, …} are given. Which number belongs to both sets?

F. 427
G. 511
H. 735
J. 780
K. 915

93. $\frac{t-1}{t-7} = \frac{2}{7}$. Find t.

A. −0.9
B. −1.4
C. −1.2
D. −1.3
E. 1.4

94. Which number in set R = $\{0.3^3, 0.3^2, \sqrt{0.3}, 0.3, \frac{1}{3}\}$ is the largest?

F. $\frac{1}{3}$

G. 0.3

H. $\sqrt{0.3}$

J. 0.3^2

K. 0.3^3

---

95. What is the ratio of the area of a regular hexagon to a regular triangle with the same side?

A. 8 : 1

B. 6 : 1

C. 6 : 3

D. 4 : 1

E. 36 : 9

---

96. ┍ ┍ ╠ ╠ ╠ ╬ ┍ ┍ ╠ ╠ ╠ ╬ ┍ ┍ ╠ ╠ ╠ ╬ . . .

If the pattern unit of the above sequence is written as a number pattern, which of the following could it be?

F. 557555

G. 557771

H. 577511

J. 115577

K. 151775

---

97. Fiona is making a bracelet. For every 2 red beads, she is using 3 green beads and 4 yellow beads. How many yellow beads does she need, if the total number of beads in the bracelet is 63?

A. 32

B. 29

C. 28

D. 20

E. 16

---

98. Set A consists of all 4–sided polygons, and set B consists of all regular polygons. Which figure does not belong to either of the sets?

F. Square

G. Equilateral triangle

H. Rhombus

J. Trapezoid

K. Right triangle

99. 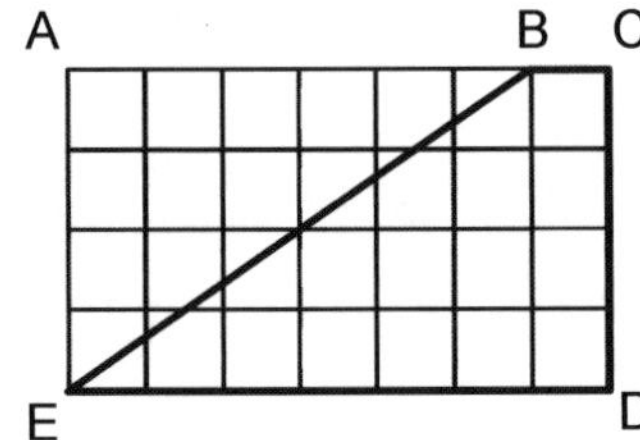

If in the diagram above, 1 small square represents 1 sq. unit, what is the area of EBCD?

A. 20 sq. units
B. 18 sq. units
C. 16 sq. units
D. 14 sq. units
E. 12 sq. units

100. If the diagonal of the square is equal to 10 inches, what is the area of the square?

F. 20 in^2
G. 36 in^2
H. 100 in^2
J. 50 in^2
K. 60 in^2

Answers

Test 6

51. E
52. K
53. D
54. F
55. D
56. J
57. C
58. H
59. D
60. F
61. E
62. F
63. D
64. J
65. C
66. J
67. D
68. J
69. B
70. K
71. C
72. F
73. C
74. H
75. B
76. J
77. D
78. J
79. C
80. F
81. B
82. G
83. B
84. K
85. B
86. H
87. E
88. J
89. A
90. H
91. C
92. G
93. D
94. G
95. B
96. J
97. D
98. J
99. D
100. J

Test 7

51. B
52. H
53. B
54. J
55. D
56. J
57. A
58. K
59. C
60. J
61. A
62. K
63. E
64. H
65. E
66. J
67. B
68. H
69. C
70. J
71. B
72. G
73. C
74. K
75. E
76. F
77. B
78. J
79. D
80. G
81. A
82. F
83. D
84. J
85. B
86. F
87. A
88. G
89. A
90. G
91. A
92. H
93. E
94. G
95. D
96. J
97. C
98. F
99. A
100. K

Test 8

51. C
52. G
53. C
54. H
55. E
56. F
57. D
58. G
59. D
60. H
61. C
62. K
63. D
64. J
65. E
66. H
67. A
68. J
69. C
70. H
71. D
72. F
73. D
74. K
75. D
76. H
77. C
78. G
79. D
80. H
81. B
82. K
83. B
84. F
85. D
86. H
87. E
88. F
89. C
90. G
91. A
92. H
93. A
94. H
95. A
96. G
97. C
98. G
99. D
100. K

Test 9

51. B
52. F
53. D
54. K
55. D
56. F
57. D
58. F
59. E
60. G
61. D
62. F
63. A
64. H
65. B
66. H
67. C
68. H
69. A
70. H
71. B
72. G
73. B
74. F
75. C
76. G
77. C
78. K
79. C
80. F
81. D
82. F
83. E
84. K
85. E
86. G
87. A
88. H
89. C
90. K
91. C
92. G
93. B
94. F
95. C
96. G
97. B
98. J
99. C
100. F

Test 10

51. A
52. J
53. E
54. F
55. C
56. F
57. A
58. J
59. B
60. H
61. A
62. G
63. E
64. F
65. B
66. G
67. A
68. F
69. C
70. K
71. A
72. J
73. C
74. J
75. B
76. G
77. C
78. G
79. D
80. F
81. B
82. F
83. D
84. G
85. B
86. F
87. E
88. J
89. B
90. F
91. E
92. H
93. B
94. H
95. B
96. G
97. C
98. K
99. C
100. J

Solutions

SHSAT Math Practice Test 6 Solutions

51. E

Since 13% of N is 72, 26% would be $2 \times 72 =$ **144**. Alternatively, we can write down an equation, since 13% = 0.13: $0.13N = 72$, or $13N = 7200$, and therefore $N = (7200 \div 13)$. Then, to find 26% of N, multiply 0.26 by $(7200 \div 13)$, getting **144**.

52. K

Surface area of a cube is the sum of areas of its sides (which are 6 congruent squares) and equal to $6a^2$, where a is the side of the square. Since it is given that $6a^2 = 600 \text{ cm}^2$, it follows that $a^2 = 100 \text{ cm}^2$, and therefore a = 10 cm. The volume of the cube is $a^3 = 10 \text{ cm}^3 =$ **1000 cm^3**.

53. D

The average of {–7,– 6 ,6– 5, . . . 6, 7, 8, 9} is (–7+ –6 + –5 + –4 + –3 + –2 + –1 + 0 + 1 + 2 +3 + 4+ 5 +6 +7 +8 + 9) ÷ 17 = **1.** This kind of the solution is correct, but rather long. It would be much faster to find just the average of the first and the last number: (–7 + 9) ÷ 2 = **1.** The average of any set of *consecutive* integers is always the same as the average of the smallest and largest member of the set.

54. F

The smallest possible perimeter is 4 + 4 + 4 = **12** (note that the problem *didn't* specify that the integers must be different).

55. D

The sum of all interior angles of any quadrilateral is 360°. ∠CBP is 20° as given. The ∠CDP is supplementary to the interior angle of the regular pentagon (which is 180°(5 – 2) ÷ 5 = 108°) and is therefore equal to 180° – 108° = 72°. The measure of the reflex angle BCD is equal to 360° – 108° = 252°. Finally, ∠BPD = 360° – (72° + 20° + 252°) = **16°**.

56. J

Step 1. 0.2 × 5 = 1
Step 2. 10 ÷ 0.1 = 100 ÷1 = 100
Step 3. 1 + 100 = **101**

57. C

0.91919191919 rounded to the nearest thousandth is equal to **0.919**,
because the next (ten–thousandths digit) of the number is 1, which is less than 5. Therefore, we should be rounding the thousandths digit down.

58. H

$a^2 - 8$ is negative if $|a| < \sqrt{8}$, which means that $-\sqrt{8} < a < \sqrt{8}$. Since $\sqrt{8} \approx 2.8$, a could be equal to –2 , –1, 0 , 1, or 2, for a total of **5 integers**.

59. D

Look at each choice individually.

A. $M \times N \times K > 0$ is false.

Counterexample: $-6 \times -4 \times -2 = -48$.

B. $M \times N \times K < 0$ is false.

Counterexample: $2 \times 4 \times 6 = 48$

C. $M + N + K = 2$ is false.

Counterexample: $4 + 6 + 8 = 18$

D. **(3M+7N+5K) is always even**, because even × odd = even, so each member of the sum is even, and therefore the whole sum is even.

E. $(M \times N \times K + 1)$ is even is false.

Counterexample: $2 \times 4 \times 6 + 1 = 49$

60. F

The possible triplets that add up to 6 are: (0, 0, 6), (0, 1, 5), (0, 2, 4), (0, 3, 3), (1, 1, 4), (1, 2, 3), and (2, 2, 2). The following three-digit numbers can be made from these triplets: 105, 150, 501, 510, 114, 141, 411, 123, 132, 312, 321, 213, 231, 204, 240, 402, 420, 222, 330, 303, 600, for a total of **21 numbers**.

61. E

Let x be the number of children's tickets, and y be the number of adult tickets. The first equation is $x + y = 25$ or, multiplying both sides by 10, $10x + 10y = 250$. From the total dollar amount and prices per ticket, we can derive the second equation $3x + 10y = 201$ ($3 per child and $10 per adult, for the total of $201). If we now subtract the second equation from the first one: $(10x + 10y = 250) - (3x + 10y = 201)$, which produces $7x = 49$. Therefore, $\mathbf{x = 7}$.

62. F

Let the side of the square QP = x. Triangle QPT is right, and therefore we can use the Pythagorean Theorem to state that $3^2 + x^2 = 6^2$. Thus, $x^2 = 27$. Since the area of the square is equal to the square of its side length, the **area of MNPQ is 27**.

63. D

Since the numbers of boys and girls can only be integers, the sum of the two parts in the ratio must be a factor of 24 in order for the ratio to be possible. The only ratio that adds up to a factor of 24 is **5 : 7**.

64. J

Let's make a table:

Pipes	Pools	Time (hrs)
5	2	2
5	1	1
1	1	5

If 5 pipes fill 2 pools in 2 hours, then they will fill 1 pool in 1 hour. But if only 1 pipe is working, it will take 5 times longer, or **5 hours** to fill 1 pool.

65. C

Let's look at a few multiples of 7: 7, 14, 21, 28, 35, 49, … . The first perfect square in this set is 49. 49 = 2 + 47 (no other pair of primes can produce an odd sum).

Therefore, a possible product is $47 \times 2 =$ **94**.

66. J

The total number of combinations for 2 tosses is equal to $6 \times 6 = 36$. The product of the two tosses will be even if at least one of the two tosses is even. This can happen in cases where the first toss is 2, 4, or 6 (6 possible second tosses for each, for a total of 18), or when the first toss is odd, but the second toss is even (first toss is 1, 3 or 5; and the second toss is 2, 4 or 6 in each of those cases, for a total of 9). $18 + 9 = 27$ possibilities that two tosses have an even product, and the probability is $27 \div 36 =$ **0.75**.

Another way to solve this: the odd product of two tosses is only possible when both tosses are odd, which can happen when the first toss is 1, 3, or 5, and the second toss is 1, 3, or 5 in each of those cases, for a total of 9. Therefore, all other tosses, $36 - 9 = 27$, are even. The probability is the same as above.

67. D

It is given that $b = -2$, and $b^{\triangle} = 3 - 5b$, $b^{\triangle} = 3 - 5(-2) = 3 + 10 =$ **13**.

68. J

If Ron made 6 mistakes, that means that he solved $30 - 6 = 24$ problems correctly. 24 out of 30 is $24 \div 30 = 0.8 =$ **80%**.

69. B

The figure has only one horizontal and one vertical line of symmetry, for a total of **2 lines of symmetry:**

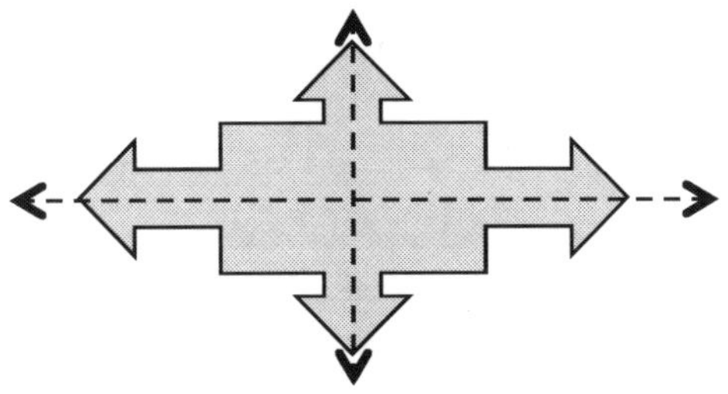

70. K

Let there be x students in class. 7 students constitute 35% of the class means that $0.35x = 7$. Therefore, $x =$ **20**.

71. C

Let the measure of angle A be y. Then, the measure of angle D is also y, and the measure of other 4 angles is $(y + 15)$ each. Since the sum of all interior angles of a hexagon is 720°, we can write the equation: $2y + 4(y + 15) = 720$. Open parenthesis and combine like terms:
$2y + 4y + 60 = 720 \rightarrow 6y + 60 = 720 \rightarrow$
$6y = 660 \rightarrow y = 110$.

That means that measure of angle A is 110°, but angle E is 15° more, which is $110 + 15 =$ **125°**.

72. F

It is given that $2a = 3b$, which means that $4a = 6b$ (multiplying both sides by 2). But it is also given that $6b = 5c$. Therefore, $4a = 5c$. Divide both sides of the equation by $4c$ and $a : c = 5 : 4$.

73. C

First, find the difference between the two numbers, because the question is about "what percentage less" is one number than the other. 200 – 70 = 130. 130 out of 200 is the same as 65 out of 100, which is **65%**.

74. H

Let Katie be x years old now, which means her brother is $(x+2)$. In 12 years her brother will be $x + 2 + 12 = x + 14$. It is also given that $x + 14 = 2x$ (twice older than his sister now). Therefore,

$x + 14 = 2x \rightarrow$ **$\mathbf{x = 14}$.**

75. B

← ↖ ↑ ↗ → ↘ ↓ ↙ ← ↖ ↑ ↗ → ↘ ↓ ↙ …

Since there are 8 units in the pattern group, divide 66 by 8 to get 6, with remainder 7. That means we should take the **7th term of the set, ↓**, as our answer.

76. J

In order to find the average of 3 numbers, we should add them up and divide the result by 3:

$((3x - 5) + (x + 2) + (2x + 6)) \div 3 =$

$(6x + 3) \div 3 =$ **$\mathbf{2x + 1}$.**

77. D

The two vertical angles are congruent to each other. The sum of interior angles of each triangle is the same (180°). Thefore, the sums of two other angles will also be equal, and we can write the equation:

$5x + 6x = 24° + 42° \rightarrow 11x = 66° \rightarrow$ **$\mathbf{x = 6°}$**

78. J

In order to be divisible by 9, a number should have the sum of all its digits be divisible by 9. The digit sum of 27,983 is 2 + 7 + 9 + 8 + 3 = 29. The closest value which is divisible by 9 and greater than 29 is 36. Since 36 – 29 = 7, **we need to add 7** to the number to make it be divisible by 9. Check: the new number is 27,983 + 7 = 27,990, its digit sum is 2 + 7 + 9 + 9 + 0 = 27, which is divisible by 9.

79. C

First, find the unit price. The price of 1 pen is $d \div n$.

If you have p dollars, you can buy p divided by the price of 1 pen, or

p ÷ (d ÷ n) = p(n / d) = pn / d or **np/d**.

80. F

Follow the proper order of operations:

1) 5 ÷ 0.1 = 50 ÷ 1 = 50
2) 8 ÷ 0.2 = 80 ÷ 2 = 40
3) 40 × 0.5 =20
4) 6 ÷ 2 = 3
5) 50 – 20 + 3 = **33**

81. B

Since the volume of the cube is equal to the third power of the length of one of the edges of the cube, $s^3 = 125$, and therefore the edge length $s = 5$. The area of each face is 5 × 5 = 25 and the surface area is, therefore, 25 × 6 = **150**.

82. G

There are 19 integers with at least one 7 between 100 and 200. The easiest way to catch them is to list them all: 107, 117, 127, 137, 147, 157, 167, 187, 197 (9 integers that don't start with '17'), and 170, 171, 172, 173, 174, 175, 176, 177, 178, 179 (10 integers). And now we need to multiply the result by 2 to find all numbers between 100 and 300 (there are 19 such integers between 100 and 200, and between 200 and 300). $19 \times 2 =$ **38.**

83. B

It is given that T and P are both negative integers. Therefore $\boldsymbol{P + T > 0}$ is **always** false because the sum of two negative numbers can never be positive.

84. K

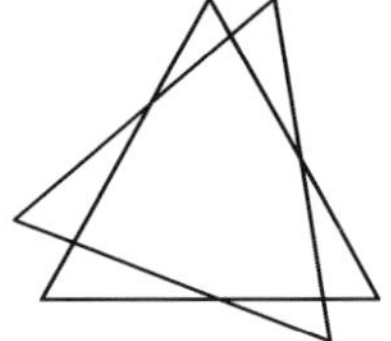

The largest number of common points for two triangles is 6, because each side could have at most 2 common points with a side of the other triangle. Therefore, two triangles cannot have **7 points** in common.

85. B

Since $t^4 = 1600$, $t^2 = 40$. t is the square root of 40, and lies **between 6 and 7,** because $6^2 < 40 < 7^2$.

86. H

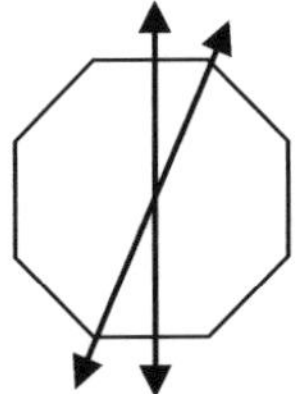

Let's take two of the closest lines symmetry of the regular octagon: the angle between them is 1/16th of the circle, which is $360° \div 16 =$ **22.5°.**

87. E

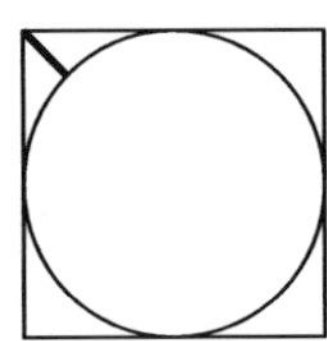

In order to find the length of the small line segment, we need to find the difference between the half of the diagonal of the square and the radius of the circle. The diagonal of the square is equal to $4\sqrt{2}$, and the circle radius is 2. Therefore, the line segment is equal to $(4\sqrt{2}) \div 2 - 2 = \mathbf{2\sqrt{2} - 2}$.

88. J

The area of each rectangle is 24 in^2. Since the shaded area is 20 in^2, the area of the overlapping part is 24 in^2 – 20 in^2 = **4 in^2**.

89. A

Since the radius of the circle is the distance between the origin and the point (–1, 1), use the Pythagorean Theorem to find the square of the radius:
$r^2 = 1^2 + 1^2 = 2$. The area of the circle is πr^2, which is equal to $\mathbf{2\pi}$**.**

90. H

Let's say that Steve entered an elevator at floor X. Then X + 7 – 8 + 3 = 10,
X + 2 = 10, and X = **8**.

91. C

Since OM = OK, angles OMK and OKM are each 45°. Since NK is perpendicular to the x-axis and angle OKM is 45°, angle NKM is 90° – 45° = 45°. Since KM = KN, angles MNK and KMN are equal, and therefore can be found using the equation (180° – 45°) ÷ 2 = **67.5°.**

92. G

It is given that $x^2y^3z^3 < 0$. The given inequality is equivalent to $(x^2y^2z^2)(yz) < 0$. For any x, y, and z, $(x^2y^2z^2) > 0$, and therefore the product ***yz* must be negative**.

93. D

The shortest way to solve the equation is to use the cross multiplication: $3(2a - 1) = 5(a + 2)$. Now open parenthesis:
$6a - 3 = 5a + 10 \rightarrow \mathbf{a = 13.}$

94. G

Since $v^2 = 16$, v could be 4 or –4. Since $w^2=49$, w could be 7 or –7. The greatest difference is equal to 4 – (–7) = 4 + 7 = **11**, when $v = 4$ and $w = -7$.

95. B

The center C of the bottom circle and points A and B form the right triangle ABC: $AB^2 = 6^2 + 6^2 = 72$ (radius of each circle is 2 cm, and AC = BC = 6 cm).
Therefore, $AB = \sqrt{72} = \mathbf{6\sqrt{2}.}$

96. J

The ratio $A : B = 4 : 7$ can be written as $A = 4p$ and $B = 7p$. Therefore, we can write $A + B = 11p$, and $B - A = 3p$. Therefore, $(A + B) \div (B - A) = 11p \div 3p$, which is **11 : 3.**

97. D

Since $4x = 3y$, $y = (4/3)x$, therefore $y > x$.
$2y = z$, which means $z > y$. $6z = v$, so $v > z$.
$7v = 8w$, meaning $v = (8/7)w$, so $v > w$.
Therefore $v > z > y > x$, and $v > w$.
Therefore, ***v* is the largest.**

98. J

The product of two sides of the rectangle must be a perfect square, because the side of the square is an integer (and therefore its area is a perfect square). Of the given pairs of numbers, only 12 and 3 multiply to a perfect square. **12 × 3** = 36.

99. D

It is given that the average of a and b is 3 times the average of c and d, which can be written as (a + b) ÷ 2 = 3((c + d) ÷ 2). Simplifying, we get: (a + b) = 3(c + d). It is also given that the average of a, b, c, and d is 10, so (a + b + c + d) ÷ 4 = 10, so (a + b + c + d) = 40. We can rewrite the sum as (a + b) + (c + d) = 40, and substitute (a + b) with 3(c + d), getting 3(c + d) + (c + d) = 40. Combining like terms, we can write 4(c + d) = 40, and c + d = 10. Now, find the average of c and d: (c + d) ÷ 2 = 10 ÷ 2 = **5**.

100. J

Since 20% of the circle is 0.2 × 360° = 72°, the angle is **72°**.

SHSAT MATH PRACTICE TEST 7 SOLUTIONS

51. B

The largest one digit number is 9, and the largest remainder it can produce is **8**.

52. H

In order to find the midpoint, find the average of the given coordinates:
$((0.1) + (-0.3)) \div 2 = -0.2 \div 2 = \mathbf{-0.1}$

53. B

Since $0.2 = 1/5$, $(0.2)^{-3} = (1/5)^{-3} = 5^3 = 125$;
$0.1 = 1/10$, $(0.1)^{-4} = (1/10)^{-4} = 10^4 = 10000$;
$125 \div 10000 = \mathbf{0.0125.}$

54. J

The total price is
($1.3 × 2) + ($3.6 × 3) = $13.40.
The total weight is 2 + 3 = 5 pounds.
Therefore the price of 1 pound is
$13.40 ÷ 5 = **$2.68.**

55. D

Since the common width of two rectangles is 3, the area of the square is 9. The area of one rectangle is (5 × 3) = 15. The total area of two rectangles is twice 15 and equal to 30. If we subtract the area of the square from 30, we will take away the overlapping part of two rectangles and will get the area of the entire figure:
30 – 9 = **21.**

56. J

If it takes 10 minutes to fill one tub, then it will take half the time, or **5 minutes**, to fill half of one tub.

57. A

Base on the given rule: $a ❄ b = a^2 - b$,
$2 ❄ -5 = 2^2 - (-5) = 4 + 5 = 9$.
Then, $9 ❄ -1 = 9^2 - (-1) = 81 = 1 = \mathbf{82.}$

58. K

$1 \text{ ft} = 12 \text{ in} \rightarrow 1 \text{ ft}^2 = 144 \text{ in}^2 \rightarrow$
$1 \text{ ft}^3 = 1728 \text{ in}^3$.
$64 \text{ in}^3 = 64 \div 1728 = \mathbf{1/27 \text{ ft}^3.}$
Alternatively, $64 \text{ in}^3 = (4 \text{ in})^3$. Since
$4 \text{ in} = (1/3) \text{ ft}$, then $(4\text{in})^3 = (1/3 \text{ ft})^3 =$
$\mathbf{1/27 \text{ ft}^3}$.

59. C

Compare formulas of areas of the given shapes: $A_{rectangle} = L \times W = L \times H$,
and $A_{trapezoid} = (1/2) \times (b_1 + b_2) \times H$.
Since the heights of the two figures are the same, and their areas are equal, the length of the rectangle must be equal to one half of the sum of the two bases of the trapezoid. Thus, L = (1/2)(k + k + 12), which equals (1/2)(2k + 12) = **k + 6.**

60. J

Let x be the number. Its reciprocal is (1/x). It is given that (1/x) = 4x. Multiply both sides of the equation by x, and get $4x^2 = 1$, or $x^2 = \frac{1}{4}$. Therefore, $\mathbf{x = \frac{1}{2}}$.

61. A

If the median of the set of 22 consecutive integers is 26.5, it implies that the two middle numbers of the set are 26 and 27 (because $26.5 = (26 + 27) \div 2$). Therefore, the first 11 numbers are 16, 17, 18, 19, 20, 21, 22, 23, 24, 25, 26. The middle number of this set is 21, so **the median is 21.**

62. K

Since $q - 10p = 0$, $q = 10p$, and $p = 0.1q$. If $p > 5$, then $0.1q > 5$. Multiply both sides of the equation by 10, and get $\boldsymbol{q > 50}$.

63. E

Since $x > y$, $z < y$, $w < z$, and $w > t$, the chain is $x > y > z > w > t$, which means that the smallest number is **t.**

64. H

Since $(5^6 + 5^6 + 5^6) = 3 \times 5^6$ and $(5^4 + 5^4 + 5^4) = 3 \times 5^{\wedge 4}$, the former divided by the latter is:
$(3 \times 5^6) \div (3 \times 5^4) = (5^6) \div (5^4) = 5^2 = \mathbf{25}$.

65. E

Triangles ACE and BDE are similar, and triangle BDE is a right triangle. First, find the hypotenuse BE:
$BE^2 = 6^2 + 8^2 = 100$, thus $BE = 10$. Then, write theproportion: AC : BD = 1.2 : 6 = AE : 10 or 1/5 = AE/10. Thus, **AE = 2.**

66. J

$4^3 = (2^2)^3 = 2^6$; $8^2 = (2^3)^2 = 2^6$.
$(2^6)(2^6) = 2^{12}$. Therefore $\mathbf{x = 12}$.

67. B

The prime factorization of 1260 is $2 \times 2 \times 3 \times 3 \times 5 \times 7$. Since $6 = 2 \times 3$, we need to select the largest factors that do not include a 2 and a 3. That's
$3 \times 3 \times 5 \times 7 = \mathbf{315}$.

68. H

Combine like terms inside of the parentheses to get $2\sqrt{11}$.
Then $(2\sqrt{11})(2\sqrt{11}) = 4 \times 11 = \mathbf{44}$.

69. C

First find the second power of the leg of either triangle by using the Pythagorean Theorem: $x^2 + x^2 = 16$, $2x^2 = 16$, $x^2 = 8$. The area of each triangle is $(1/2)x^2 = 4$. Finally, the total area of the figure is
$8 \times 2 + 2 \times 4 = \mathbf{24}$.

70. J

Follow the proper order of operations:
$[32 \div (-8) \times 2] - [24 \div 4 \times (-3)] - 1 =$
$[(-4) \times 2] - [6 \times (-3)] - 1 = -8 + 18 - 1 =$
$10 - 1 = \mathbf{9}$.

71. B

The angle that is supplementary to the angle x is at the same time equal to the 167° angle, because BC and DE are parallel and thus the two angles are corresponding. Therefore, angle x is $180° - 167° = \mathbf{13°}$.

72. G

Only **four** distinct 3-digit numbers can be made with these digits: 102, 120, 201, 210, because we can use each digit only ones and 0 cannot be the first digit.

73. C

To find the smallest positive difference between the 3–digit number and 2–digit number, we need to take the smallest 3–digit number and the largest 2–digit number. These are 100 and 99, respectively. Therefore $100 - 99 = \mathbf{1}$.

74. K

$RQ = 3\sqrt{2}$ in is the diagonal of the cube face. Let s be the edge of a cube. Then, by Pythagorean Theorem, $s^2 + s^2 = (3\sqrt{2})^2 = 9 \times 2 = 18$. $2s^2 = 18$, therefore $s^2 = 9$ in^2 and s = 3 in. The perimeter of the shaded face is therefore 4 × 3 in = **12 in.**

75. E

There are 7 units between two given points. In order to find the length of one unit, Find the distance between two points and divide it by 7:

$$\frac{1}{4} - (-\frac{5}{8}) = \frac{2}{8} - (-\frac{5}{8}) = \frac{7}{8}; (\frac{7}{8}) \div 7 = \frac{1}{8}.$$

Now we can find the coordinate of the point V: $\frac{1}{4} + \frac{2}{8} = \frac{1}{4} + \frac{1}{4} = \frac{2}{4} = \mathbf{\frac{1}{2}}$.

76. F

Use the Pythagorean Theorem to find RQ: $RQ^2 = 17^2 - 8^2 = 289 - 64 = 225$, therefore $RQ = \sqrt{225} = 15$. The perimeter of the entire figure is $2(8 + 15) = \mathbf{46}$.

77. B

Since it is given that the ratio of a to c is 3 to 7, we can let a = 3x, and c = 7x. Then, $3c = 3 \times 7x = 21x$ and $7a = 7 \times 3x = 21x$. The ratio of $3a$ to $7c$ is 21x to 21x or just **1 : 1.**

78. J

If $3x - 5y + 17 = 2$, then $3x - 5y = 2 - 17$, which is –15. Next, take the equation $3x - 5y = -15$ and multiply both sides by –1, getting: $5y - 3x = \mathbf{15}$.

79. D

Use the Pythagorean Theorem to write $c^2 = a^2 + b^2$. Since $a + b = 9$, it follows that $(a + b)^2 = a^2 + 2ab + b^2 = 9^2 = 81$. Since $ab = 16$, $a^2 + 2(16) + b^2 = 81$. Therefore, $a^2 + b^2 = 81 - 32 = 49$. $c^2 = 49$, and $\mathbf{c = 7}$.

80. G

The perimeter of the figure DOEF consists of a pair of equal line segments: DO = OE = 5/2 (as radii of the circle), line segment FD (tangent to the circle), and line segment FE, whose length is the difference between the lengths of segments FC and EC. Since the measure of angle F is 30°, the hypotenuse FC of the right triangle FDC is twice the leg CD and is equal to 10, and FD = $5\sqrt{3}$ (special 30°–60°–90° triangle). Since the measure of angle DCF is 60° and OC=OE, triangle COE is equilateral, with CE=OC=OE=5/2. The perimeter of DOEF is therefore equal to OD + OE + FE + DF = OD + OE + (FC–EC) + DF = 2.5 + 2.5 + (10–2.5) + $5\sqrt{3}$ = **12.5 + $5\sqrt{3}$.**

81. A

The worst case scenario is that we get only pennies. We would have to have a minimum of **11 pennies** to have more than 10 cents.

82. F

Let the original price be p dollars. Last year's price can be written as $p + 0.2p = 1.2p$. This year's price is: $1.2p - (0.2 \times 1.2p) = 1.2p + 0.24p = 0.96p$. $0.96p = 192$ (that's given). Therefore, $p = 192 \div 0.96 = 19200 \div 96 =$ **$200.**

83. D

Since 11 years from today James will be 26 years old, today he's 26 – 11 = 15 years old. Sam is 3 times older, which is 15 × 3 = **45**.

84. J

Since the triangle is isosceles, its sides are either [6 cm, 6 cm, 12 cm] or [6 cm, 12 cm, 12 cm]. Its sides cannot be [6 cm, 6 cm, 12 cm] because 6 + 6 = 12, so that triangle does not exist. Therefore, the perimeter is 6 + 12 + 12 = **30 cm.**

85. B

Since 99.999 = 100 – 0.001, and $100 - 100^c = 99.999$, we can say that $100^c = 0.001 = 10^{-3}$. 100^c can be written as 10^{2c}. We have $10^{2c} = 10^{-3}$, thus 2c = –3, and **c = –1.5.**

86. F

The total distance is 3 × 60 + 2 × 55 = 290 miles, and the total time is 3 + 2 = 5 hours. The average rate is therefore 290 ÷ 5 = **58 mph**.

87. A

Notice that the set of perfect cubes 1, 8, 27, 64, **125**, 216, . . . consists of all numbers which are 2 less than each number of the given set. Therefore, the missing number is 125 + 2 = **127.**

88. G

Since the radius R of either circle is 4/2 = 2, the base of the triangle ABC is equal to 2R = 4, and the height is 3R = 6. The area of ABC = (1/2) × base × height = (1/2) × 4 × 6 = **12.**

89. A

If $(x-1)^4 = 16$, then $(x-1)$ could be equal to 2 or –2. Therefore, x could be 2 + 1 = 3 or –2 + 1 = –1. $(x-5)$ could be 3 – 5 = –2 or –1 – 5 = –6. **–6** is one of the answers.

90. G

Let's make a table:

Machines	Items	Time (hrs)
10	200	4
5	200	8
5	100	4
5	300	8 + 4 = 12

If it takes 10 machines 4 hours to produce 200 items, it will take 5 machines 8 hours to produce 200 items. It will take 5 machines 4 hours to produce 100 items. It will therefore take 5 machines **12 hours** to produce 300 items.

91. A

Let the radius of the small circle be *r*. Then the radius of the large circle is 2*r*. The area of the big circle is $4\pi r^2$ and the area of the small one is πr^2. The shaded area is $4\pi r^2 - \pi r^2 = 3\pi r^2$. $3\pi r^2$ out of $4\pi r^2$ is $\mathbf{\frac{3}{4}}$.

92. H

n	1	2	3	4	5	6	7	8
Term	3	8	13	18	23	28	33	38

The term is T(n) = 5n – 2 . Therefore, T(60) = 5 × 60 – 2 = 298, and T(70) = 5 × 70 – 2 = 348. 348 – 298 = **50.** Alternatively, the pattern is add 5 to each term to get the next term. Then, the difference between the 70th and 60th terms is: (70 – 60) × 5 = 10 × 5 = **50.**

93. E

Pick a number from the range, for example –0.5, and check it:

I. –0.5 < 0.25 is true,

II. –0.5 < –0.125 is true,

III. –0.125 < 0.25 is true.

Alternatively, for (I), x is always negative, and x^2 is always positive, so it's always true. For (II), x^3 is always closer to 0 than x, since x is between 0 and -1, and for (III), x^3 is always negative, and x^2 is always positive.

94. G

Between 1 and 50, each group of 10 has one digit 3, and one digit 7 in it, except the set of 30 – 39, Which is 30, 31, 32, 33, 34, 35, 36, 37, 38, 39 and have 11 threes. The total is 5 sevens + 4 threes + 11 threes = **20.**

95. D

Use the formula of the area of trapezoid to write the equation:

A = 7 × (6 + 6 + a + 5) ÷ 2 = 77. Solve for a: (17 + a) ÷ 2 = 11 → 17 + a = 22 → a = **5.**

96. J

The largest two digit prime number is 97, and the smallest two digit prime number is 11. 97 – 11 = **86.**

97. C

A line segment from point M to point K will form four congruent triangles. The area of each of these triangles is $24 \div 4 = 6$ cm^2. Since the parallelogram AMNK consists of two of these triangles, its area is $6 \times 2 =$ **12 cm^2.**

98. F

If $11x = \sqrt{16} + \sqrt{49} = 4 + 7 = 11$, then $x = 11 \div 11 =$ **1.**

99. A

If the average of 5 numbers is 6, then their sum is $6 \times 5 = 30$. Note that we do not need to know the product: that's extraneous information and it's there to distract you.

100. K

Since the sum of two consecutive integers A, and B is t, the sum of the next two integers C, and D will be $t + 4$, because C = A + 2, and D = B + 2. The total increase of the sum is 4.

SHSAT Math Practice Test 8 Solutions

51. C

$27 - x = 18 - y$ is given. Add x to the both sides of the equation: $27 = 18 + x - y$. Then, if both sides of the equation are divided by 3, the equation will become $9 = x - y$, which gives the equivalent equation $x - y =$ **9**.

52. G

$(\sqrt{9} + \sqrt{36})^2 = (3+6)^2 = 9^2 =$ **81.**

53. C

The Greatest Common Factor of 24 and P is 8, so P must be a multiple of 8. Among the provided choices, the only multiple of 8 is **16.**

54. H

Each side of the triangle must be less than the sum of two other sides and greater than their difference. Since $11 = 1 + 10 = 2 + 9 = 3 + 8 = 4 + 7 = 5 + 6$, the largest possible side of the triangle will be **7 cm**, because $7 < 4 + 4$ is true. For any other combination, with numbers greater than 7, triangle does not exist (for example, $8 < 3 + 4$ is false).

55. E

The operation ۞ is defined for all nonzero numbers by k ۞ $t = -k^2 - t$.

5 ۞ $-24 = -5^2 - (-24) = -25 + 24 = -1$.

-1 ۞ $2 = -(-1)^2 - 2 = -1 - 2 =$ **−3.**

56. F

The temperature at 6 AM is 18°F . The temperature 6 hours later is −18°F. The temperature change per hour is (−18 − (18))°F ÷ 6 hours = **−6°F per hour.**

57. D

In the interval between – 7 and 1.9, there are **8** one–digit integers: −6, −5, −4, −3, −2, −1, 0, and 1.

58. G

20% = 0.2 = 1/5.

3/8 of 240 is (3/8) × 240 = 90.

1/5 of 90 is 90 ÷ 5 = **18.**

59. D

$(2x - 3) \div x = x + 5$. If each side of the equation is multiplied by x, the new equation will be $2x - 3 = x^2 + 5x$. If $2x$ is then subtracted from both sides and 3 is added to both sides of the equation, the new equation will be $x^2 + 3x + 3 =$ **0.**

60. H

If p is a positive integer, then $2p(2p + 1)(2p - 1)$ is always divisible by 6, because these three numbers are consecutive: $(2p - 1)$, $2p$, $(2p + 1)$, at least one of them is even, and at least one of them is a multiple of 3. So, the product of those two numbers will always be **divisible by 6**. For example, the product of the numbers 4, 5, and 3 is always divisible by 6 because 4 times 3 is 12.

61. C

Since $h - 5g = 0$, $h = 5g$. It is given that $h < 20$, thus $5g < 20$, **or $g < 4$.**

62. K

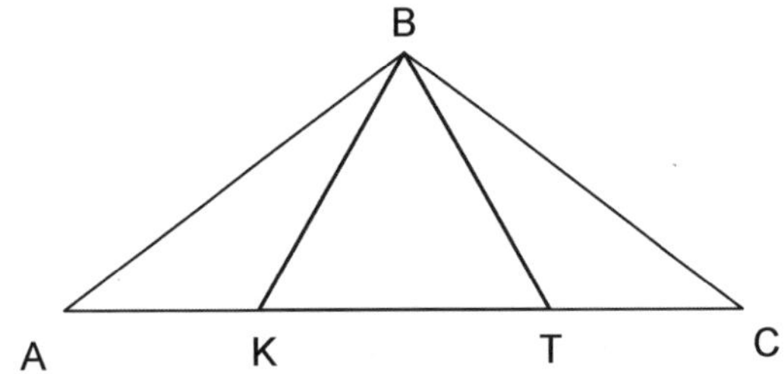

Triangle KBT is equilateral, so $\angle BKT = 60°$, and supplementary angle BKT is $180° - 60° = 120°$. Since $\angle KAB = 15°$, to find the measure of angle ABK: $180° - 120° - 15° = 45°$.

63. D

Since $A=3B$, and all variables are positive, $A > B$. $A = 0.25C$, which means $C = 4A$ and $C > A$. $0.25C = 0.1D$, meaning $D = 2.5C$ and $D > C$. $0.1D = E$, which means $D = 10E$, and $D > E$. Thus, we have $D > C > A > B$ and $D > E$. That means that **D is the largest.**

64. J

The new figure looks like this:

The lengths of the removed segments are the same as the lengths of the added segments, which means that the perimeter did not change:
$P = 2(11 + 5) =$ **32 cm**

65. E

Only 17 is divisible by 17, because it itself is a prime number. Any other number than 17 which is divisible by 17 will have more than 2 factors and will not be a prime.

66. H

The degree measure of angle MON is equal to the 2/5 of the circle, which is $(2/5) \times 360° =$ **144°.**

67. A

If 20% of a price is \$120, the total price is $120 \times 5 = \$600$. Since \$120 has already been paid, the amount left to pay is $\$600 - \$120 =$ **\$480.**

68. J

$7 < 3g - 1 \leq 17$. Add 1 to each part of the inequality, producing $8 < 3g - 1 \leq 18$. Now, if each part of the inequality is divided by 3, We'll get $8/3 < g \leq 6$.
Four integers will satisfy this inequality: **3, 4, 5, and 6.**

69. C

The pattern group has 9 items:
⊕ ⊖ ⊗ ⊘ ⊙ ⊚ ⊛ ⊜ ⊖

The shape in the 111th place will be ⊗, because 111 ÷ 9 = 12r3, and the 3rd figure in the pattern group is ⊗.

70. H

The total number of marbles is 10. Black marbles with even numbers are: 0, 2, 4. $P_{\text{Even black marble}}$ = 3 out of 10 = **0.3.**

71. D

The average of three numbers is 7, which means that their sum is 3 × 7 = 21. Average of the other three numbers From the same set is 11, which makes their sum 3 × 11 = 33. The sum of the whole set is, therefore, 54. The average of all 6 numbers is 54 ÷ 6 = **9.**

72. F

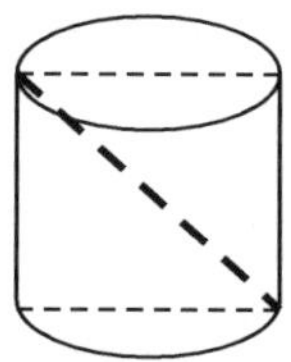

If the radius of the cylinder base is 4 and the height of the cylinder is 6, the longest distance between the point on the top circumference and the point on the base circumference of the cylinder is the diagonal of the rectangle which divides the cylinder into two halves. To find the distance, use the Pythagorean Theorem: $d^2 = 6^2 + (2 \times 4)^2 = 36 + 64 = 100$. Therefore, **d = 10.**

73. D

The sum of p consecutive integers is 3. The possible sets of consecutive integers that add up to 3 are: [3], [1, 2], [0, 1, 2], [–2, –1, 0, 1, 2, 3]. The lengths of these sets are 1, 2, 3 and 6, respectively. Of these possibilities, the answer **6** is available.

74. K

A bus travels 130 miles in 2 hours and the next 200 miles in 4 hours. (200 miles ÷ 50 mph). 130 + 200 = 330 miles is the total distance and 2 + 4 = 6 hours is total time. The average rate is, therefore, 330 ÷ 6 = **55 mph.**

75. D

The ratio of k to q is 7 to 9. $k : q = 7 : 9$, so q ÷ k = 9 : 7. $7q \div 3k$ is the same as (7/3)(q/k) = (7/3)(9/7) = 3 : 1.

76. H

If 40 is 40% of 40% of an integer, we can write an equation: (0.4)(0.4)(N) = 40 or 0.16N = 40. Multiple both sides of the equation by 100: 16N = 4000 → **N = 250.**

77. C

Since the diameter of the circle is 2, the radius is 1, and the area of the circle is $\pi(1)^2 = \pi$. The area of the shaded region is the difference between the area of the rectangle and the semicircle: A = (2)(1) – π/2 = **2 – 0.5π.**

78. G

Since $(a+a)^2 = (2a)^2 = 4a^2$, we can conclude that $4a^2 = 4a^{5-3x}$ or $a^2 = a^{5-3x}$ and $2 = 5 - 3x$. The solution to this equation is $\mathbf{x = 1}$.

79. D

A box contains 7 red balls and 2 blue balls. When B blue balls are added, the probability to get a red ball will be: $7 \div (7 + 2 + B)$ and must be equal to 0.5. It means that $7 + 2 + B = 14$, and $\mathbf{B = 5}$.

80. H

$1 - 0.999 = 10^{-3n}$ is given. Since $1 - 0.999 = 0.001 = 10^{-3}$, we conclude that $10^{-3n} = 10^{-3}$. Therefore, $\mathbf{n = 1}$.

81. B

Between 12 and 77, there are **13** multiples of 5, because $77 - 12 = 65$, and $65/5 = 13$.

82. K

Let's rewrite 2.5 as an improper fraction $\frac{5}{2}$. Now it is not difficult to find the reciprocal, which is $\frac{2}{5}$ or $\frac{4}{10} = 0.4$.

83. B

In order to find the largest possible difference $C - B$, we need to take the largest possible B and the smallest possible C. Since the tens digit of C is less than 6, and the ones place of B is greater than 5, the largest C is 59, and the smallest B is 16. The difference between these two numbers is $59 - 16 = \mathbf{43}$.

84. F

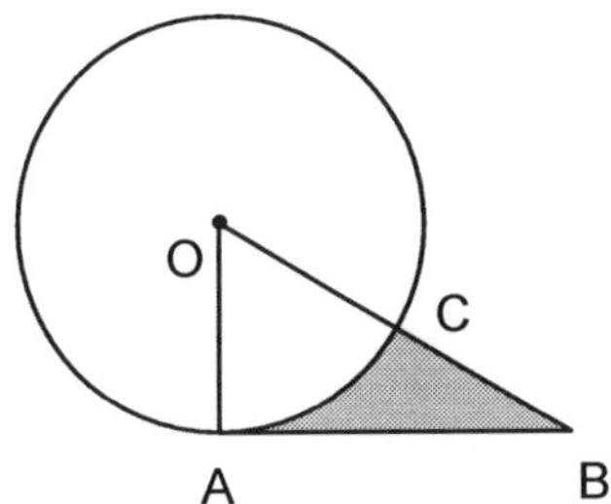

AB is a tangent to the given circle O with radius 6, and $\angle ABO = 30°$. Triangle OAB is a special 30°–60°–90° triangle, which means that $AB = 6\sqrt{3}$. The area of the triangle OAB is $(1/2)(6)(6\sqrt{3}) = 18\sqrt{3}$. The area of the sector AOC is 2/6ths of the area of the circle, which is $36\pi/6$ or 6π. The area of the shaded region is therefore $\mathbf{18\sqrt{3} - 6\pi}$.

85. D

A package of postcards costs \$40. An individual postcard costs \$0.85. The simple division will allow us to find the answer: 4000 cents ÷ 85 cents = 47*r*5. Therefore, if you buy **47 postcards**, you will pay 5 cents less than the price of a package.

86. H

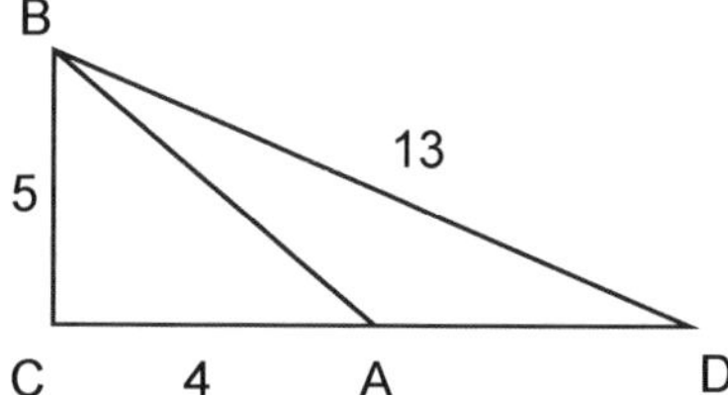

Since DBC is a right triangle, and the point A lies on the line segment CD, using the Pythagorean Theorem, we can find CD: $CD^2 + 5^2 = 13^2$, CD = 12.
AD = 12 – 4 = **8.**

87. E

If the average speed is 20 mph for a 60 mile trip, the time spent on the trip is 60 ÷ 20 = 3 hrs. For the return trip, the time spent is 60 ÷ 30 = 2 hrs. The total time is 3 + 2 = 5 hrs. The total distance is 120 miles. The average speed is, therefore, 120 ÷ 5 = **24 mph.**

88. F

Let's place the pattern into the table:

n	1	2	3	4	5	6	Number of term
N	4	7	10	13	16	19	The term itself

From the pattern, notice that N = 3n + 1. Now in order to find the 100th term, substitute n with a 100:
N(100) = 3 × 100 + 1 = **301.**

89. C

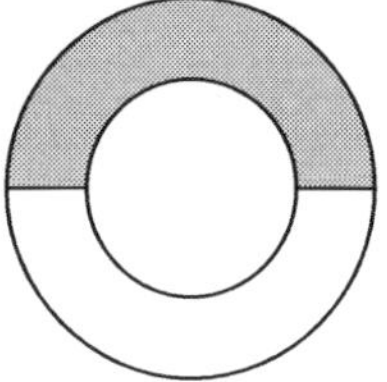

The radius of the large circle is 10, and the width of the space between the circles is 4. This implies that the area of the large circle is 100π. The radius of the small circle is 10 – 4 = 6, which means that the area of the small circle is 36π. The area of the space between the circles is then $100\pi - 36\pi = 64\pi$. Finally, the area of the shaded part is 64 ÷ 2 = **32π.**

90. G

Since the average of six consecutive integers is 12.5, the two middle integers in the set are 12 and 13. The set is 10, 11, 12, 13, 14, 15. The next 6 consecutive integers are: 16, 17, 18, 19, 20 and 21. Their average is (1/2)(18 + 19) = **18.5.**

91. A

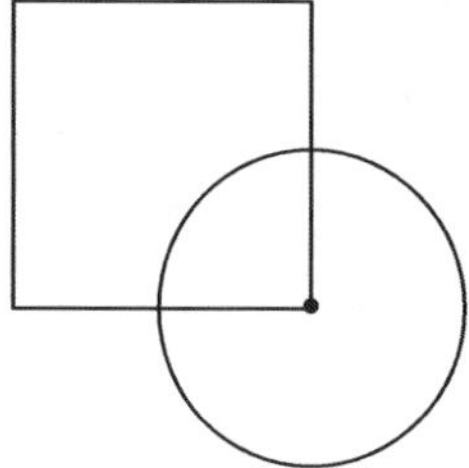

The area of the circle is 4π. A quarter of the circle overlaps the square: $\frac{1}{4}$ of 4π is π, and the part of the circle that lies outside the square is 3π. Since the area of the square is 16, the total area of figure is **$16 + 3\pi$.**

92. H

The side of square Q is the square root of 25, which is 5. It follows that the perimeter of Q is 5 × 4 = 20 in. Therefore, the perimeter of P is 20 – 4 = 16 in. The side of P is 4, which is 16 when squared. Therefore, the area of square P is **16 in^2.**

93. A

The key to quickly solving this problem is to realize that one of the bases of the triangle, the line segment between points (2, 7) and (8, 7) is horizontal and parallel to the x-axis. The length of that line segment is just the difference of its endpoints' x-coordinates: 8 – 2 = 6. The height of the triangle is the length of the line segment that starts at point (20, 9) and is perpendicular to the extended base and ends on it (at some point whose y-coordinate is 7). The length of that segment is 9 – 7 = 2. Therefore, the area of the triangle is (1/2)(6)(2) = **6.**

94. H

x^3 x^2 x

Since $x^3 < x^2 < x$, x must be a positive fraction less than 1, which is $\mathbf{\frac{3}{8}}$.

95. A

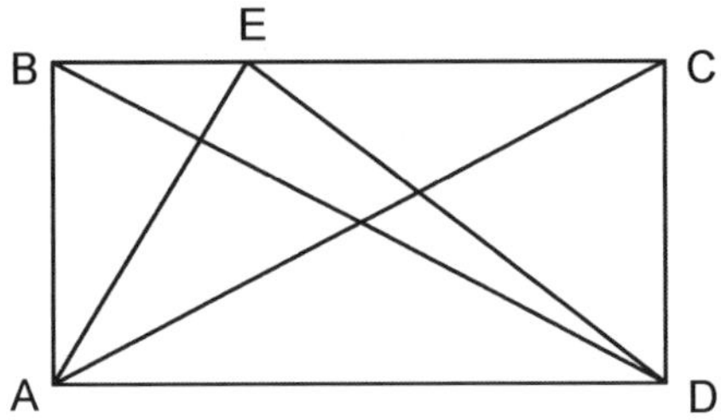

Triangles ABD and AED have the same base AD and the same height, which is the distance between BC and AD. Triangles ABC and BCD have the same base BC (BC = AD) and the same height, which is the distance between BC and AD. Therefore, these four triangles have the same area. **Triangle AEC**, however, has a smaller base, and therefore a different area.

96. G

Let the number of students in grade 8B be N. Since their average score is 87, the sum of their scores is 87 × N = 87N. There are twice as many students in grade 8A, which means there are 2N students, and since their average is 90, the sum of their scores is 90 × 2N = 180N. The sum of scores of all students is 87N + 180N = 267N, and the total number of students is N + 2N = 3N. In order to find the average of all scores, divide the sum of all scores 267N by 3N and get **89**.

97. C

Let's say that Nick has X nickels and Y quarters. Then X + Y = 32 and the total value of all coins can be expressed as 5X + 25Y = 460 cents. Divide both sides by 5 in the second equation to get X + 5Y = 92. Then, subtract the second equation from the first one to get that 4Y = 60, meaning that Y = 15. Keep in mind, however, that Y represents the number of quarters. To get the number of nickels, subtract 15 from 32, to get **17 nickels.**

98. G

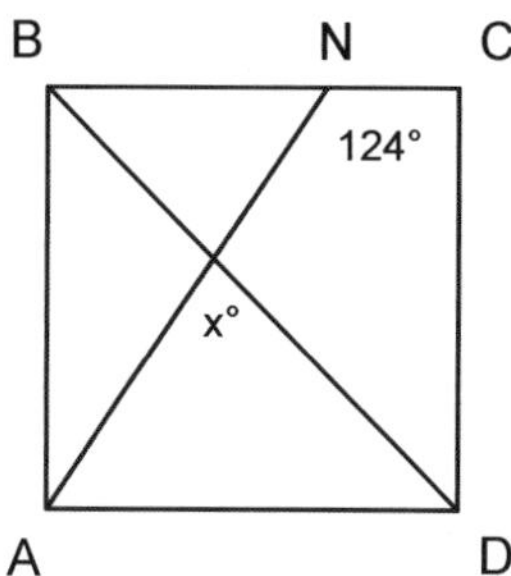

Since BC parallel to AD, angle NAD and angle ANC are supplementary

As corresponding angles and the measure of NAD = 180° – 124° = 56°. BD is a diagonal of the square and the measure of angle BDA is 45°. Now to find the measure of angle x, just use the sum of all interior angles of any triangle:

x + 45° + 56° = 180°. Therefore, **x = 79°**.

99. D

Let's make a table:

Workers (W)	Days (D)
3	20
1	60
4	15

Since the relationship between W and D varies inversely, if W divided by 3, we need to multiply D by 3 and when we multiply W by 4, we need to divide D by 4. Thus, we first find out how many days it takes one worker to do the job (60 days), and then divide that by 4 to figure out how many days it takes 4 workers to do the job. The answer is **15 days.**

100. K

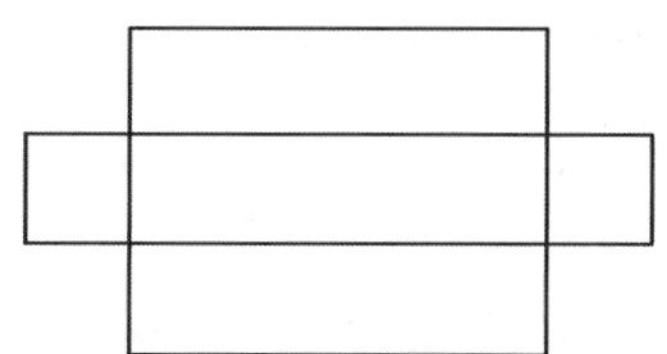

If we mark the individual line segments as shown in the diagram above, we can deduce that a = (12 – 8) ÷ 2 = 2, and b = (6 – 2) ÷ 2 = 2. The total perimeter is P = 4a + 4b + 2 × 2 + 2 × 8 = 8 + 8 + 4 + 16 = **36**.

A faster way to solve is to notice that the whole figure looks like a rectangle with cutout corners. Since cutting out corners in this manner doesn't change the overall perimeter of the rectangle, you can add up the original sides of this rectangle, which is 12 by 6, to get 2(12 + 6) = **36.**

SHSAT Math Practice Test 9 Solutions

51. B

Since $3m(2 - 12) - 2m(3 + 12) = 0$, it follows that $3m(-10) - 2m(15) = 0 \rightarrow -30m - 45m = 0$, and finally: $-75m = 0$. Now divide both sides of the equation by -75 to get $\mathbf{m = 0}$.

52. F

Since the circumference is 1, an arc that's $\frac{2}{5}$ units long is $\frac{2}{5}$ths of the circumference. That means that the central angle corresponding to this arc is $\frac{2}{5}$ of 360°. $(\frac{2}{5})(360°) = \mathbf{144°}$.

53. D

Since 1 pear costs as much as 5 onions, 3 pears cost as much as 15 onions. But 2 oranges cost as much as 3 pears, so 2 oranges cost as much as 15 onions. Therefore, 4 oranges will cost twice as much, which is the same as **30 onions.**

54. K

Let the side of the square is T. Then the diameter of a circle is also T. The perimeter of the square is 4T, and the circumference of the circle is πT (remember that T is the diameter, which is twice the radius). The ratio of the perimeter of the square to the circumference of the circle is 4T : πT, which is **4 : π.**

55. D

$\mathbf{1^1, 2^4, 3^9, 4^{16}, \ldots, 9^n}$

Notice, that the base of each term is an integer, and the power of each term is the is the square of the base. Therefore, $n = 9^2 = \mathbf{81}$.

56. F

Every hour, the cars will be closer to each other by (24 + 36) = 60 miles. Therefore, they will meet in 5 hours, since $300 \div 60 = 5$. If they started at 1 PM, they will meet at **6 PM.**

57. D

Note that the diagonal of the square is the diameter of the circle, due to symmetry. It follows that The circumference of the circle is **36π.**

58. F

Since $m = 0.2n$ and $n = 2.5k$, replace n with $2.5k$ to get: $m = 0.2(2.5k)$, then $m = 0.5k$. This means that m is **0.5** of k.

59. E

It is given that $16^2 = 8^{3-x}$. In order to solve the equation, make the base the same for both sides by substituting 16 with 2^4 and 8 with 2^3: $(2^4)^2 = (2^3)^{3-x}$. Now apply the properties of the exponents to produce: $2^8 = 2^{9-3x}$. Now that the two sides of the equation have the same base, we can conclude that $8 = 9 - 3x \rightarrow 3x = 1$, which implies that $\mathbf{x = \frac{1}{3}}$.

60. G

To visualize the problem, create a Venn diagram:

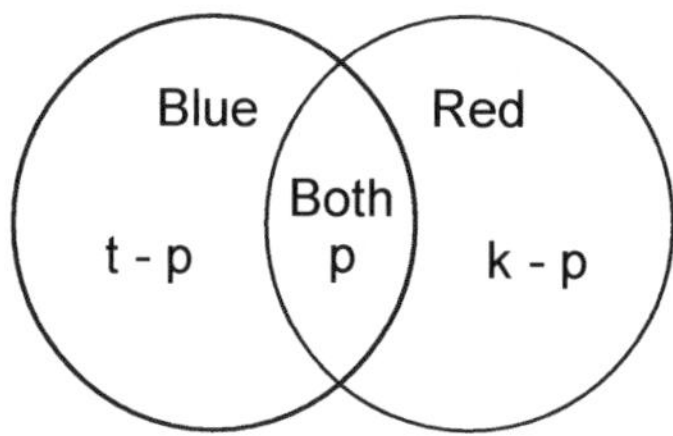

Now to find the total number of students, add all parts: t – p + p + k – p = t + k – p. It is given that t + k – p = 24, which means the total number of students is **24.**

61. D

Let's examine just the triangle by using the given facts:

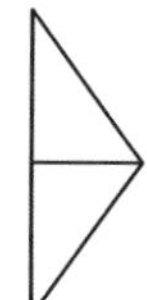

Note that the median (shown in the figure) of the isosceles triangle is also its height. That means that both of the two halves of the triangle are right, and therefore the height is equal to 3 (the Pythagorean triple 3, 4, 5). Now find the area of the isosceles triangle (1/2)(8)(3) = 12 and add to the area of the rectangle to produce A = 12 + (8)(12) = 12 + 96 = **108.**

62. F

Since triangle ABD is equilateral, the measure of angle ABE is 60°. Triangle ABC is isosceles and the measure of angle BCA is the same as the measure of angle BAE and equal to 25°. The measure of angle BEC is the sum of 25° and 60°, because the angle BEC is an exterior angle of the triangle BAE, and equal to the sum of the two angles of the triangle that are not adjacent to it, which is **85°.**

63. A

Since $v > t$, $q < v$, $q > p$, $t < p$, it's possible to rewrite the set of inequalities as a chain: $v > q > p > t$. Now it is visible that **v is the largest.**

64. H

The angle with the measure of $3y$ is an exterior angle of the right triangle, so $90° < 3y < 180°$, or $30° < y < 60°$. Among the provided choices, only $\boldsymbol{y = 35}$° satisfies the inequality.

65. B

The sum of two odd integers is always even. There exists only one even prime number – it's 2. 2 = 1 + 1, which means there's only **1** such prime number.

66. H

All interior angles of a regular pentagon are equal, which means that the measure of angle MLN is 540° ÷ 5 = 108° (the sum of all interior angles of any pentagon is

180°(5 – 2) = 540°). The triangle MLN is isosceles, because all sides of the regular pentagon are equal, and ML = NL. The measure of the angle LNM is therefore (180° – 108°) ÷ 2 = 36°. The angle MNK is the supplementary for the angle LNM and is 180° – 36° = **144°**.

67. C

a% of *b* is always the same as *b*% of *a*, because *a*% of *b* is (*a*/100)(*b*) = *ab*/100 and *b*% of a is (*b*/100)(*a*) = *ba*/100 = *ab*/100. The result of the division of the number by itself is 1. The quotient is 1 and when multiplied by 5 is equal to **5.**

68. H

The inequality $8 \le |3g - 1| \le 11$ is equivalent to two inequalities:
$11 \le 3g - 1 \le -8$ and $8 \le 3g - 1 \le 11$.
Solve each of the inequalities:
$-10 \le 3g \le -7$ and $9 \le 3g \le 12 \rightarrow$
$-10/3 \le g \le -7/3$ and $3 \le g \le 4$.
The first inequality has only one integer solution (–3), the second inequality has two integer solutions (3 and 4). The total number of integer solutions is therefore **3.**

69. A

The right triangle formed by any of the four corners of the rectangle has a hypotenuse of 13 and a smaller leg of 5 (half of the shorter diagonal of the rhombus). Use the Pythagorean Theorem to find the other leg: $13^2 - 5^2 = 169 - 25 = 144$. Therefore, the leg is 12, and the length of the rectangle is *twice* that, or 24 cm. The width of the rectangle is equal to the small diagonal of the rhombus, which is 10 cm. The area of the rectangle is therefore 10 × 24 = **240 cm²**.

70. H

The total number of marbles is 12. White marbles with a prime number on them are 11, 5 and 19. Therefore, the probability is equal to 3 marbles out of 12, which is 3/12 or $\mathbf{\frac{1}{4}}$.

71. B

Since the average of five distinct positive integers is 20, their sum is 20 × 5 = 100. In order for the largest number to be as large as possible, the smallest numbers in the set must be as small as possible. It's known that the median is 12, and since there are 5 numbers in the set, 12 must be the third number. The first two numbers should therefore be 1 and 2 (two smallest distinct positive integers), giving us: 1, 2, 12, _ , _. In order to get the largest possible number at the end of the set, we need to find the smallest possible number for the 4th position in the set. That number must be bigger than 12 (because 12 is the median), and the smallest such number is 13, giving us: 1, 2, 12, 13, _. Now, since we know the sum of the numbers, we can deduce the largest number:
100 – (1 + 2 + 12 + 13) = 100 – 28 = **72.**

72. G

The sum of two sides of the triangle is $7 + 8 = 15$. The length of the third side must be less than 15, and must be an integer. The largest integer less than 15 is 14. The largest possible perimeter is therefore $15 + 14 =$ **29.**

73. B

$4^{17} + 4^{17} + 4^{17} + 4^{17} = 4 \times 4^{17} = 4^{17+1} = 4^{18}$

$4^{18} = (2^2)^{18} = \mathbf{2^{36}}$.

74. F

Use the distributive property for the given expression:

$3(a - 5) - 2(1 - 4a) - (11a + 6) =$

$3a - 15 - 2 + 8a - 11a - 6 = -23$,

The terms with a as a factor cancel each other out because $3a + 8a - 11a = 0$, which leaves us with $-15 - 2 - 6 =$ **−23.**

75. C

If the ratio of p to q is 2 to 3, then the ratio of q to p is 3 to 2. It follows that the ratio of q^2 to the $3p^2$ is 9 to (3×4) or 9 to 12. The simplest form of that ratio is **3 to 4**.

76. G

12% of 300 oz is $0.12 \times 300 = 36$. Therefore, there are 36 oz of acid in the mixture. If 100 oz of water evaporates, the total amount of mixture will be $300 - 100 = 200$ oz, but it will contain the same 36 oz of acid. 36 out of 200 is the same as 18 out of 100 (36/200 = 18/100). Therefore, the new acid content is **18%.**

77. C

The dimensions of the entire solid rectangular prism are 4, 4, and 8. Let the length of the longest diagonal HE be d.

$d^2 = 4^2 + 4^2 + 8^2 = 16 + 16 + 64 = 96$,

therefore HE = d = $\sqrt{96} = \mathbf{4\sqrt{6}}$**.**

78. K

If x and y are two different integers, and $x^2 = 4$, and $y^2 = 49$, x could be equal to 2 or −2 and y could be 7 or −7. The largest possible value for $y - x$ is $7 - (-2) =$ $7 + 2 =$ **9.**

79. C

It is given, that the volume of the box is 35 and each dimension is an integer. There are two possible integer triplets that multiply to 35: $1 \times 5 \times 7$, and $1 \times 1 \times 35$. Since we are told the dimensions are distinct, they must 1 by 5 by 7. From the diagram, it is apparent that the dimensions of the cutout squares, which correspond to the height of the box, are the smallest of the three dimensions, which is 1. Therefore, before 1 square unit was cut out of each corner of the board, the length of the board was $7 + 1 + 1 = 9$, and the width was equal to $5 + 1 + 1 = 7$. Thus, the perimeter of the original cardboard was $2(9 + 7) =$ **32.**

80. F

Take a look at the trapezoid CABD:

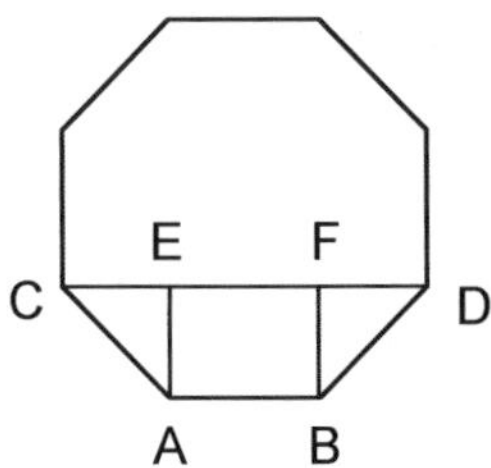

Draw AE perpendicular to CD and BF perpendicular to CD. It's easy to see that AB = EF = 2 (side length of the octagon is given). Each interior angle of the regular octagon is 135° (180° × (8 – 2) ÷ 8 = 135°). It follows that CAE and DBF are both isosceles triangles, because the measure of angle CAE is 135° – 90° = 45°. Since the octagon is regular and its side is 2, CA = AB = BD = 2. Now, for the special triangles CAE and DBF, we can conclude that CE = AE = BF = FD = $\sqrt{2}$. Finally, CD = CE + EF + FD = **$2\sqrt{2}$ + 2.**

81. D

The perimeter of the square PQRT is 4, which means that each side of the square is 1. Since QV is the hypotenuse of the right triangle formed by the corner of square, QV > 1 (because one of the legs of the triangle is 1, and the hypotenuse is always larger than either of the legs). For the triangle QVT (not given) the interior angle QVT is an obtuse, and in this triangle QV < QT. But QT is the diagonal of the square and equal to $\sqrt{2}$. Therefore, 1 < QV < $\sqrt{2}$. Among the provided choices, only **1.3** satisfies this inequality.

82. F

It is given that $a + b = 29$, $b + c = 37$, and $a + c = 42$. Add all left sides of the equations and all right sides to get $2a + 2b + 2c = 108$. Divide both sides by 2 to get $a + b + c = 54$. The average of a, b, and c is (a + b + c) ÷ 3 = 54 ÷ 3 = **18.**

83. E

Let m and n be the two numbers. We know that the sum of their reciprocals is $1/m + 1/n = (m + n) / (mn) = 2$. Simplify the equation by multiplying both sides by mn: $m + n = 2mn$. Since $mn = 23$, $m + n =$ **46.**

84. K

The largest side of the triangle ABC is BC, because this side is opposite to the largest angle. In triangle BCD, the largest side is BD, because it is opposite to the obtuse angle of the triangle. Therefore BD > BC, and **BD** is the longest.

85. E

The answer is **none**, because the left side of the equation $4p + 6q = 13$ is the sum of two even integers, which makes it an even integer that cannot be equal to 13, which is odd.

86. G

The smallest possible value of x^2 is 0, attained when $x = 0$. Since 0 is between –2 and 6, we need to find the value of y for $x = 0$, which is –3.

87. A

The 120° angle is an exterior angle of the triangle BED, so 120° is equal to the sum of the two remote angles of this triangle, one of which is a right angle. Therefore, the measure of angle EBD is equal to $120° - 90° = 30°$. The measure of angle ABC is equal to $180° - (130° + 30°) = 20°$. Since x is an exterior angle of the triangle ABC, $x = 90° + 20° =$ **110°.**

88. H

Let's make a table:

position	1	2	3	4	5	6	7
term	0	1	4	9	16	25	36

Each term is equal to the square of the position of the previous term. Therefore, 15th term will be equal to $(15 - 1)^2 = 14^2 =$ **196.**

89. C

Let the radius of the small circle is r and the radius of the large be R. It is given that $\pi r^2 = 25\%$ of πR^2, or $\pi r^2 = (1/4)\pi R^2$. Divide both sides by π and multiply by 4: $4r^2 = R^2$, and $R^2 \div r^2 = 4$. Take the square root of both sides to get the needed ratio: R : r = **2 : 1**.

90. K

-7 is $\frac{1}{3}$ of -21. $-\frac{1}{3}$ is $\frac{1}{3}$ of -1. 1 is $\frac{1}{3}$ of 3; $\frac{1}{3}$ is $\frac{1}{3}$ of 1. The answer is therefore $\mathbf{\frac{1}{2}}$, because if $\frac{1}{2}$ is $\frac{1}{3}$ of N, then N must be equal to $\frac{3}{2}$, which is not an integer.

91. C

Let the side of each square be V. The perimeter of the entire figure will be $P = V + 7V + V + 7V = 16V$. It is given that P = 96 cm, therefore $16V = 96$, and V = 6 cm. The area of each square is therefore $6 \times 6 =$ **36 cm^2**.

92. G

Let Denny be D years old. Then Ann is D + 24 years old. In 10 years, Ann will be (D + 24 + 10) and Denny will be (D + 10) years old. But we also know that she'll be 3 times as old as Denny. Express that as an equation: $(D + 24 + 10) = 3(D + 10)$ or $D + 34 = 3D + 30$. Therefore, D = 2. Ann is 24 years older, which means she is **26**.

93. B

Graph the line:

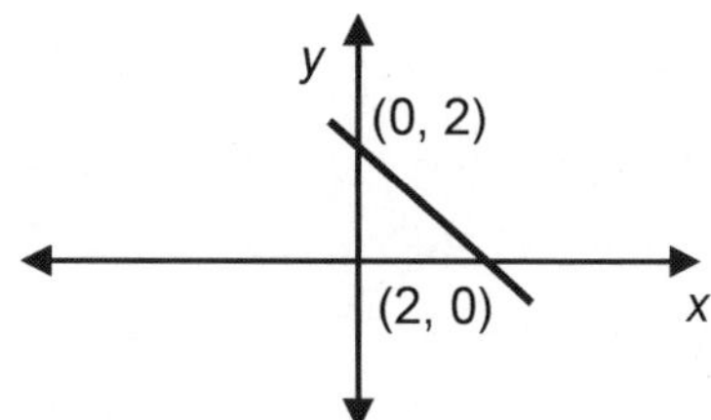

The line forms an equilateral right triangle with the x–axis and the y–axis. The area of the triangle is $(1/2)(2)(2) =$ **2.**

94. F

Since $x^3 < x$, x must be a negative number or a positive fraction. But $x^2 > x$, which means it is not a fraction. $(\mathbf{-2})^3 = -8$ and $(-2)^3 < -2 < (-2)^2$, because $-8 < -2 < 4$.

95. C

The average of $(2a + b)$, $(3a - 2b)$, and $(4a + b)$ is 12, which means that $((2a + b) + (3a - 2b) + (4a + b)) \div 3 = 12$. Simplifying that gets us: $2a + b + 3a - 2b + 4a + b \div 3 = 12$, or $9a \div 3 = 12$. Therefore, $9a = 36$, and $\boldsymbol{a} = \mathbf{4}$.

96. G

All of the available choices are small integers. It's given that $y^2 = 5x^2 + 11$, so we can try a few small values of x to see how that changes y. Trying $\boldsymbol{x} = \mathbf{1}$ produces $y^2 = 16$ and $y = 4$, which is one of the choices. (For $x = 2$, $y^2 = 39$, which makes $y > 6$).

97. B

Call the two numbers C and N, and use a system of equations based on the given data: C + N = 26 and C – N = 12. Add the two equations to get: 2C = 38, which means C = 19 and N = 7. **19** is the larger number.

98. J

Call the three dimensions of the box L, W and H. We have: L × W = 15, W × H = 21, and L × H = 35. Multiply all left sides and all right sides of the equations:
L × W × W × H × L × H = 15 × 21 × 35
$(LWH)^2 = 3 \times 5 \times 3 \times 7 \times 5 \times 7 =$
$(3 \times 5 \times 7)^2$. Therefore, the volume of the box is L × W × H = 3 × 5 × 7 = **105 in^3**.

99. C

Jim can paint the wall in 6 hours. That means he can paint 1/6th of the wall per hour. John can paint the same wall in 12 hours, meaning that his rate is 1/12th of the wall per hour. Together they can paint 1/6 + 1/12 = 3/12 = 1/4th of the wall per hour, which means that together they can paint the wall in **4 hours.**

100. F

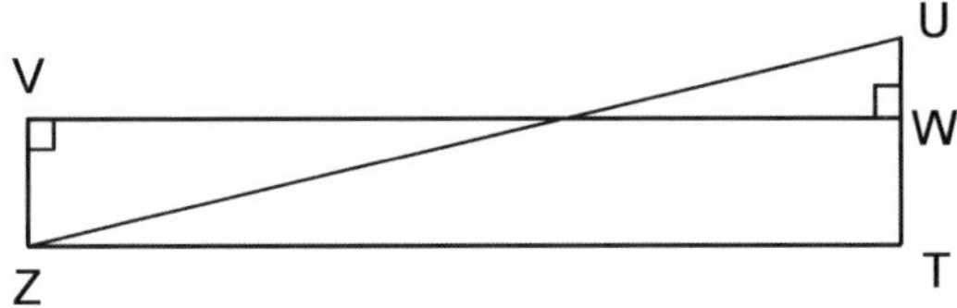

Connect Z and U and extend UT to the intersection with ZT, which is parallel to VW. Now we have: UT = 6 + 4 = 10; ZT = VW = 24. Use the Pythagorean Theorem to find ZU: $ZU^2 = 24^2 + 10^2 = 576 + 100 = 676$. **ZU = 26**.

SHSAT Math Practice Test 10 Solutions

51. A

The smallest prime number is 2, and the largest negative integer is –1. Their product is 2 × (–1) = **–2**.

52. J

The even integers between –7 and 7 are –6, –4, –2, 0, 2, 4, and 6, for a total of **7 integers.**

53. E

Jane has 200 – 108 = 92 pages left and Kevin has 80 pages left. 92 is 12 more than 80 (92 – 80 = 12). Find what percent of 80 is 12: (12/80)(100) = **15%.**

54. F

Since the operation ▶◀ is defined for all nonzero numbers by ▶X◀ = 3X – 1, we can write that ▶5◀= 3 × 5 – 1 = 14 and that ▶–7◀ = 3 × (–7) – 1 = –21 – 1 = –22; ▶5◀ + ▶–7◀ = 14 + (–22) = **–8.**

55. C

Since the scale factor of the two similar hexagons is 2 (each side of the big hexagon is twice as large as each side of the small hexagon), the area of the large hexagon will be 4 times larger than the area of small hexagon (area scales as a square of the dimensions). Therefore, the area of the large hexagon will be (3 sq. in) × 4 = **12 sq. in.**

56. F

$\sqrt{169} = 13$; $\sqrt{144} = 12$; $\sqrt{N} = 13 - 12 = 1$.
$N = 1^2 = \mathbf{1}$.

57. A

Since 8 is in the ten–thousandths place and 8 > 5, we need to add 1 to the value of the thousandths place. 98.9998 is thus approximately equal to **99.000**. Do not forget to keep the 3 digits after the decimal point.

58. J

Each group of 4 mice has 3 gray mice and 1 white mouse. There are 5 groups of 4 in the set of 20 mice. The total number of grey mice is therefore 5 × 3 = **15.**

59. B

It is given that 3 + (1 ÷ *x*) = 2. Subtract 3 from both sides of the equation to get (1 ÷ *x*) = –1. Therefore, ***x* = –1.**

60. H

A number that is divisible by 3, but not divisible by 6 should be odd (because 6 is 2 × 3; if it's divisible by 3, but not by 6, that means that 2 is not one of its factors). To quickly check if a number is divisible by 3, you can test whether the sum of all its digits is divisible by 3. Write down the smallest odd 3–digit numbers: 101, 103, 105, 107, ... It's clear that **105** is the smallest number which satisfies both conditions.

61. A

It is given that $a(a - b) = 117$ and $ab = 52$. Using the distributive property, the first equation can be written as $a^2 - ab = 117$. Since $ab = 52$, $a^2 - 52 = 117$. Solve for a: $a^2 = 117 + 52 = 169$, and $a = \sqrt{169} =$ **13.**

62. G

The two parts of the arithmetic expression (29.8)(17.9) – (29.8)(7.9) have a common factor 29.8. Use the inverse of the distributive property to get:
$(29.8)(17.9) - (29.8)(7.9) =$
$29.8(17.9 - 7.9) = 29.8 \times 10 =$ **298.**

63. E

The total number of marbles must be divisible by 15, because if there are $7x$ of red and $8x$ of green marbles, the total number of marbles is $15x$. Among the available choices, only **30** is divisible by 15.

64. F

If the sum of 7 consecutive odd numbers is 91, then the middle number is $91 \div 7 = 13$ (the middle number in a set of evenly spaced numbers with an odd number of terms is the average of the set). Now, place all numbers in order: 7, 9, 11, 13, 15, 17, 19, and find the sum of the two largest terms: $17 + 19 =$ **36.**

65. B

An odd number of negative factors will produce a negative product. The largest odd number which is less than 8 is 7. Therefore, there can be at most **7** negative numbers.

66. G

The largest possible value of the expression $-|3 - x|$ is 0, achieved when $x = 3$. For any other x, $|3 - x|$ will always be positive and therefore the negative of it will always be negative. The largest value of the entire expression is **5**, because $-|3 - x| + 5 = 0 + 5 =$ **5.**

67. A

Since $A > B$, $C < A$, $D < B$, and $E = D$, make two chains: $A > B > C$ and $A > B > D = E$. It is now clear that **A** is the largest number.

68. F

The given figure has a point of symmetry, but does not have any line of symmetry.

69. C

The difference between Kevin's and Eli's scores is $96 - 80 = 16$. The question can then be restated as follows: 16 is what percent of 80? The answer is $(16/80) \times 100\% =$ **20%.**

70. K

For the set of integers {2, 3, 7, X, 9}, if 7 is the median of the set, X could be 7, 8, or 9, because in an ordered set of integers with an odd number of terms, the median is the middle number. Therefore, the answer **cannot be determined** with the given information.

71. A

Express the given facts algebraically: let the side of the square be h: Perimeter P = 4h, and the area is h^2. It is given that numerically $h^2 = 2(4h)$, or h^2 = 8h. Since h is not equal to 0, h must be **8** to make the equation true.

72. J

Let Danny have P quarters and P pennies. The total amount of money in cents is: 25P + 1P = 26P. This number must be divisible by 26. The only answer whose cent value is divisible by 26 is **$7.80.**

73. C

If ABCD is a square with the area of 16 cm^2, then the side of the square is 4 cm. If DE is one fourth of AD, then DE = 1 cm, and AE = 4 – 1 = 3 cm. ABE is a right triangle, and therefore its area is equal to (1/2) × 4 × 3 = 6 cm^2. Therefore, the area of the DEBC is equal to the difference between the area of the square and the area of the triangle ABE, which is 16 – 6 = **10 cm^2.**

74. J

Call the proper fraction N. Its reciprocal is 1/N. It is given that N + 1/N = 2.9. The fastest way to solve the problem now is to check each of the available answers:

1/2 + 2/1 = 2.5

1/3 + 3/1 > 3

2/3 + 3/2 =13/6 < 2.9

2/5 + 5/2 = 29/10 = 2.9, therefore $\mathbf{\frac{2}{5}}$ is the proper fraction.

75. B

Let's rewrite the given sequence of numbers 12112111211112... as a set of groups of 2, 3, 4, 5, etc. numbers:

12 112 1112 11112 111112 ...

Let's figure out how many groups we have before the 44th term, by adding up their lengths: 2 + 3 + 4 + 5 + 6 + 7 + 8 + 9 = 44. The 8th group is 111111112, because each group has as many ones as the order of the term: 8th group has 8 ones and one 2. Therefore the sum of all digits from 40th to 44th is the sum of four 1s and one 2. That's 1 + 1 + 1 + 1 + 2 = **6.**

76. G

The average of 2b, 5b, 7b, and 10b is equal to (2b + 5b + 7b + 10b) ÷ 4 = 24b ÷ 4 = **6b.**

77. C

Since KLMN is an isosceles trapezoid with LM = KN an $\angle M = 42°$, we can find the measures of all interior angles of the trapezoid, because the measures of the angles MLK and NKL are the same and equal to $180° - 42° = 138°$. The angle NKX is supplementary to the angle NKL (or it is an alternate interior angle for angle MNK) and therefore equal to 42°. The sum of all interior angles of any triangle is 180°, so $42° + 88° + \angle X = 180°$, which means that $\angle \mathbf{X} = \mathbf{50°}$.

78. G

Divide the given number 109,456 by 7 and find the remainder: $109{,}456 \div 7 = 15{,}636r4$. That means our number is 4 more than the number that is divisible by 7. So, $109{,}456 - 4 = 109{,}452$ is divisible by 7. But the question is: "What is the smallest integer that can be added to 109,456 to make the result divisible by 7?" Next multiple of 7 after 109,452 is $109{,}452 + 7 = 109{,}459$ is divisible by 7. Therefore the given number 109,456 need a **3** added to it to get 109,459.

79. D

Assume that each bag going through the security checkpoints is numbered in order: 1, 2, 3, 4, etc. A bag will be checked twice only if its number is divisible by 3 and by 4, which means it must be divisible by 12. $200 \div 12 = 16r8$. Therefore, **16** bags will be checked twice.

80. F

Multiply both sides of the equation $2x^2 - 3x = 5$ by 2 to get $4x^2 - 6x = 10$.
Take the equation $4x^2 - 6x = 10$ and add 1 to the both sides: $4x^2 - 6x + 1 = 10 + 1$.
Finally $4x^2 - 6x + 1 = 11$.

81. B

If place all points on the coordinate plane, triangle ABC will have the horizontal base AB [$AB = 2 - (-1) = 3$] and vertex C, which is 2 units from the base AB, therefore the height of the triangle is 2. Now we can find the area $(1/2)(3)(2) = 3$.

82. F

If $Y = 2C - 3X$, then $2C - 3X = Y$. Add $3X$ to both sides of the second equation: $2C = 3X + Y$ and then divide both sides by 2: $\boldsymbol{C = 0.5(3X + Y)}$.

83. D

In order to find the greatest integer of the set, first find the sum of all integers. The sum is $11 \times 4 = 44$. To maximize the value of the 4th integer, the first three need to be as small as possible. The three smallest possible positive integers are: $1 + 2 + 3 = 6$. The 4th integer will therefore be $44 - 6 = \mathbf{38}$.

84. G

The angle DEP is the supplementary to the angle of CEP, which is one half of an angle of the equilateral triangle. The measure of angle DEP is thus equal to $180° – (1/2) \times 60° = 180° – 30° =$ **150°.**

85. B

Since the probability of picking a red chip from the box is 0.2, there are $0.2 \times 25 = 5$ red chips in the box. If we want to increase the probability to 0.5, we need to add X red chips to the box. That means that (5 + X) out of (25 + X) must be equal to 0.5. Write the equation as follows: $(5 + X) = 0.5(25 + X)$. Multiply both sides of the equation by 2 and solve it: $10 + 2X = 25 + X \rightarrow$ **X = 15**.

86. F

The diagonal of the octagon is its line of symmetry, and therefore bisects the angle it originates from. The sum of all interior angles of an octagon is 180(8 – 2). Therefore, each interior angle of the regular octagon is equal to $(180(8 – 2) \div 8) = 135°$. To find the missing angle, divide that by 2: $135° \div 2 =$ **67.5°.**

87. E

If $-6 \leq x \leq -4$ and $4 \leq y \leq 6$, xy will always be negative (since x is always negative and y is always positive). To make it as small as possible, we want to pick the most negative value of x, and the most positive value for y. Therefore, we want to pick x = –6 and y = 6, making xy = **–36.**

88. J

Let's solve the inequality:
$3d – 5 < 7 \rightarrow 3d < 12 \rightarrow d < 4$.
The largest possible d is **3.**

89. B

State the given information as an equation: $\pi R^2 = 5(2\pi R) \rightarrow R^2 = 10R$. Since R > 0, divide both sides by R to get **R = 10.**

90. F

During the first 120 miles of a 240 mile journey, a truck driver maintained an average speed of 50 mph, and therefore spent $120 \div 50 = 2.4$ hours. Since the average speed of the entire trip was 60 mph, his total time was $240 \div 60 =$ 4 hours. That means that the time spent on the second half of the trip was $4 – 2.4 = 1.6$ hours. Since the second half of the trip was also 120 miles long, his average speed on the second half had to be $120 \div 1.6 =$ **75 mph**.

91. E

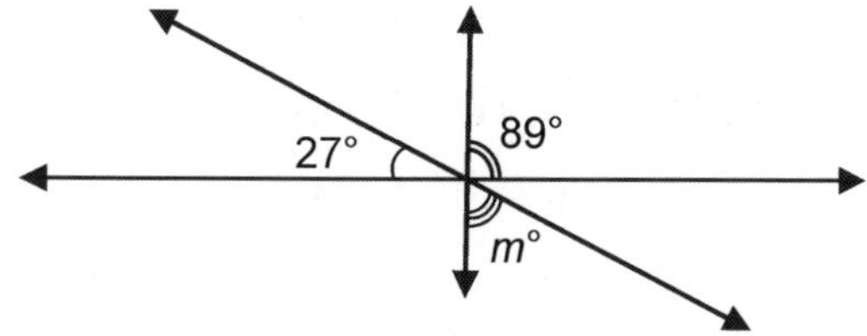

The angle between the 27° and the 89° angles is also equal to $m°$. Since together the angles form a line, we can write the equation $27° + m° + 89° = 180°$. Solve for $m°$ to get **m = 64**°.

92. H

M is the set of multiples of 5 and N is the set of multiples of 7. The numbers that belong to both of the sets are those that are divisible by 5 and by 7. Among the choices, **735** is such a number.

93. B

To solve the equation, use the cross product: $7(t-1) = 2(t-7)$. Expand that to get: $7t - 7 = 2t - 14$. Combine like terms to get $7t - 2t = -14 + 7 \rightarrow 5t = -7 \rightarrow$ $t = -7/5 \rightarrow$ $\mathbf{t = -1.4}$.

94. H

Since 0.3 is a fraction, $0.3^3 < 0.3^2 < 0.3$, but $\sqrt{0.3} > 0.5$. Therefore, $\mathbf{\sqrt{0.3}}$ is the largest number in the set.

95. B

The regular hexagon consists of 6 regular (equilateral) triangles with the same side. Therefore, the ratio is **6 : 1**.

96. G

The main pattern set is ┍ ┍ ╟ ╟ ╟ ╫ and consists of 6 figures: the first two the same, the next three the same, and the 6th is unique. Among the provided choices, the number set with the same pattern is **557771**.

97. C

The pattern set consists of 9 beads: 2 red beads, 3 green beads and 4 yellow beads. The total of 63 beads will have $63 \div 9 = 7$ groups of 9. Each group will have 4 yellow beads. Therefore, the total number of yellow beads is $4 \times 7 =$ **28.**

98. K

A right triangle is not a 4–sided polygon (it has 3 sides), nor is it regular, because the hypotenuse is always larger than either of its legs.

99. C

EBCD is a trapezoid with bases of lengths 1 unit and 7 units, and a height of 4 units. The area of the trapezoid is therefore equal to $(1/2)(4)(1 + 7) =$ **16**. Another way to do this is to recognize that the entire figure is a rectangle with the area $4 \times 7 = 28$, and ABE is a triangle with the area $(1/2)(4 \times 6) = 12$, so EBCD has the area is $28 - 12 =$ **16.**

100. J

Let B be the side of the square. Then, $B^2 + B^2 = 10^2 \rightarrow 2B^2 = 100$, and $B^2 =$ **50.** But B^2 is the area of the square, which is what the problem asks for.

Made in the USA
San Bernardino, CA
10 July 2015